My Life
With Jesus Christ

By _____

Covering My Life from _____ to

My Life Verse_____

_____

_____

The Verse for this Season in My Life _____

_____

_____

As I enter into this season of my life, these are my thoughts
and prayers _____

_____

_____

_____

_____

_____

_____

_____

_____

_____

_____

_____

_____

_____

_____

_____

_____

_____

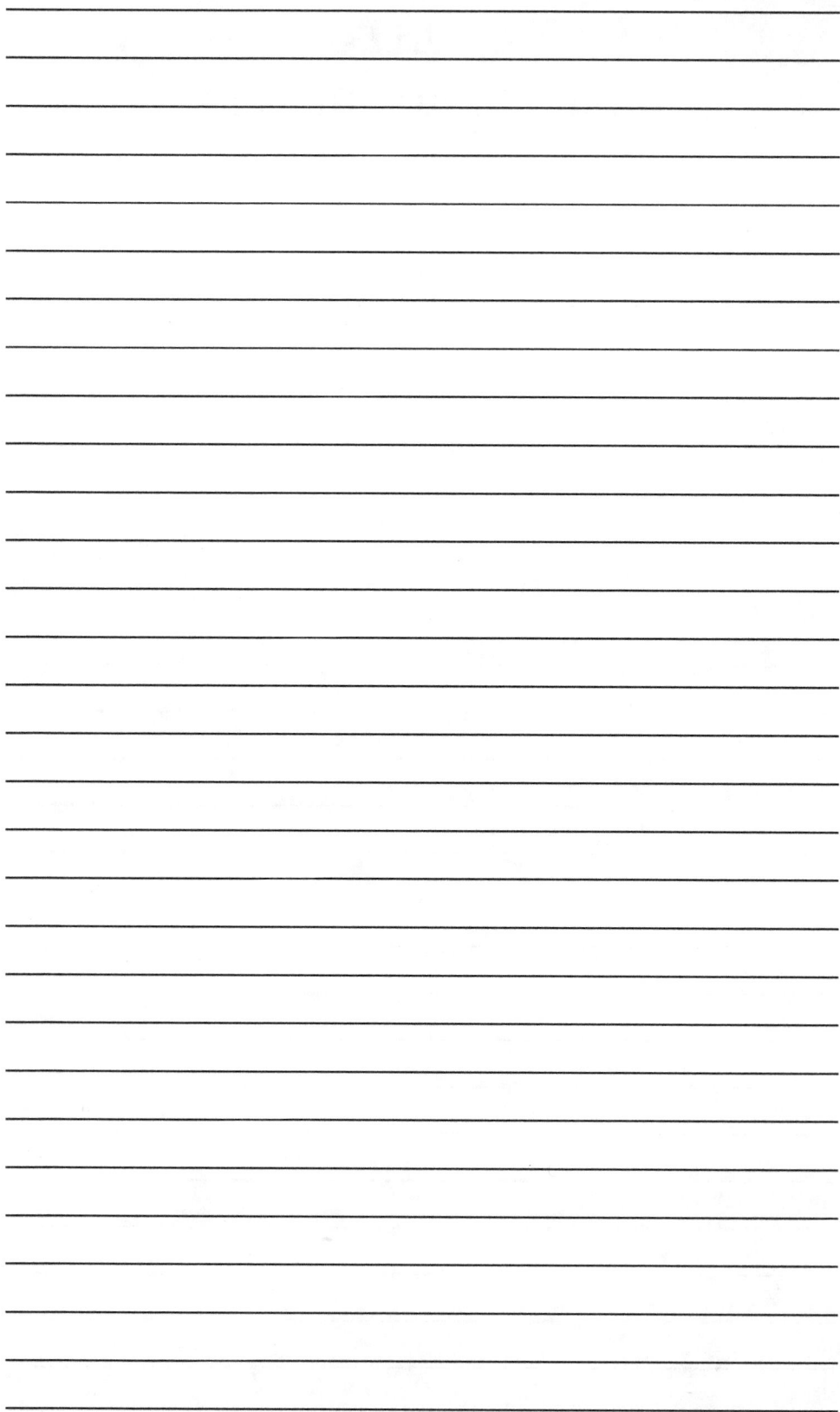

Date: _____

Memory Verse For The Week

_____

_____

_____

_____

My Thoughts Regarding This Verse

_____

_____

_____

_____

_____

_____

_____

_____

_____

_____

_____

_____

_____

_____

_____

_____

_____

_____

Today I Am Grateful For:

_____

_____

_____

_____

_____

Daily Reading

_____

_____

_____

_____

_____

_____

_____

Today's Prayer

Man ought always to pray

_____

_____

_____

_____

_____

_____

_____

_____

_____

_____

Today I Am Grateful For:

_____

_____

_____

_____

_____

Daily Reading

_____

_____

_____

_____

_____

_____

_____

Today's Prayer
Man ought always to pray

_____

_____

_____

_____

_____

_____

_____

_____

Today I Am Grateful For:

_____

_____

_____

_____

_____

Daily Reading

_____

_____

_____

_____

_____

_____

_____

Today's Prayer
Man ought always to pray

_____

_____

_____

_____

_____

_____

_____

_____

_____

Today I Am Grateful For:

_____

_____

_____

_____

_____

Daily Reading

_____

_____

_____

_____

_____

_____

_____

Today's Prayer
Man ought always to pray

_____

_____

_____

_____

_____

_____

_____

_____

_____

Today I Am Grateful For:

_____

_____

_____

_____

_____

Daily Reading

_____

_____

_____

_____

_____

_____

_____

_____

Today's Prayer
Man ought always to pray

_____

_____

_____

_____

_____

_____

_____

_____

_____

Today I Am Grateful For:

_____

_____

_____

_____

_____

Daily Reading

_____

_____

_____

_____

_____

_____

_____

Today's Prayer
Man ought always to pray

_____

_____

_____

_____

_____

_____

_____

Today I Am Grateful For:

_____

_____

_____

_____

_____

Daily Reading

_____

_____

_____

_____

_____

_____

_____

Today's Prayer
Man ought always to pray

_____

_____

_____

_____

_____

_____

_____

_____

_____

Teaching

Date_____   Speaker_____

Bible Verse _____

Topic _____

_____
_____
_____
_____
_____
_____
_____
_____
_____
_____
_____
_____
_____
_____
_____
_____
_____
_____
_____
_____
_____
_____
_____
_____
_____
_____
_____
_____

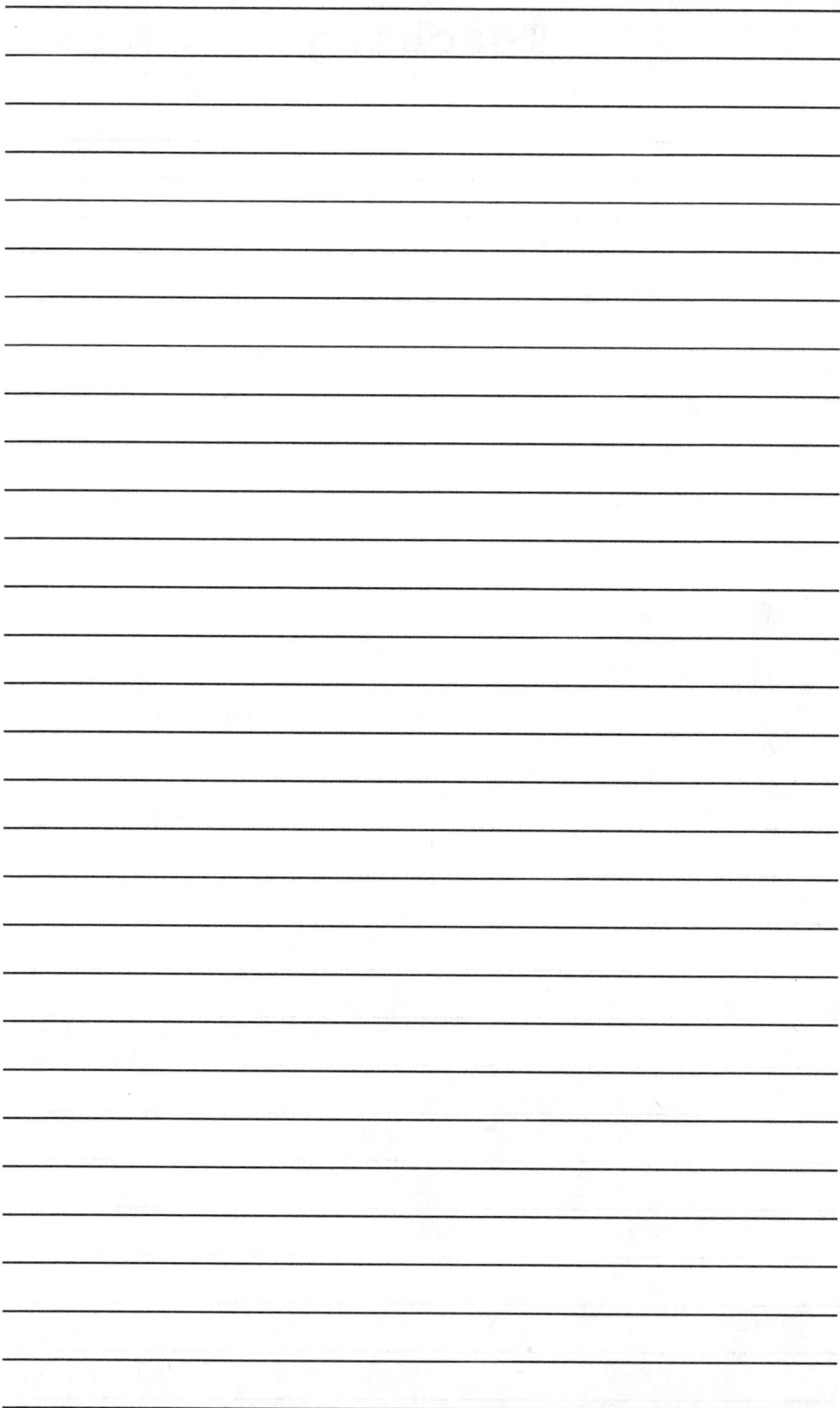

Teaching

Date_____   Speaker_____

Bible Verse _____

Topic _____

_____
_____
_____
_____
_____
_____
_____
_____
_____
_____
_____
_____
_____
_____
_____
_____
_____
_____
_____
_____
_____
_____
_____
_____
_____
_____
_____
_____
_____

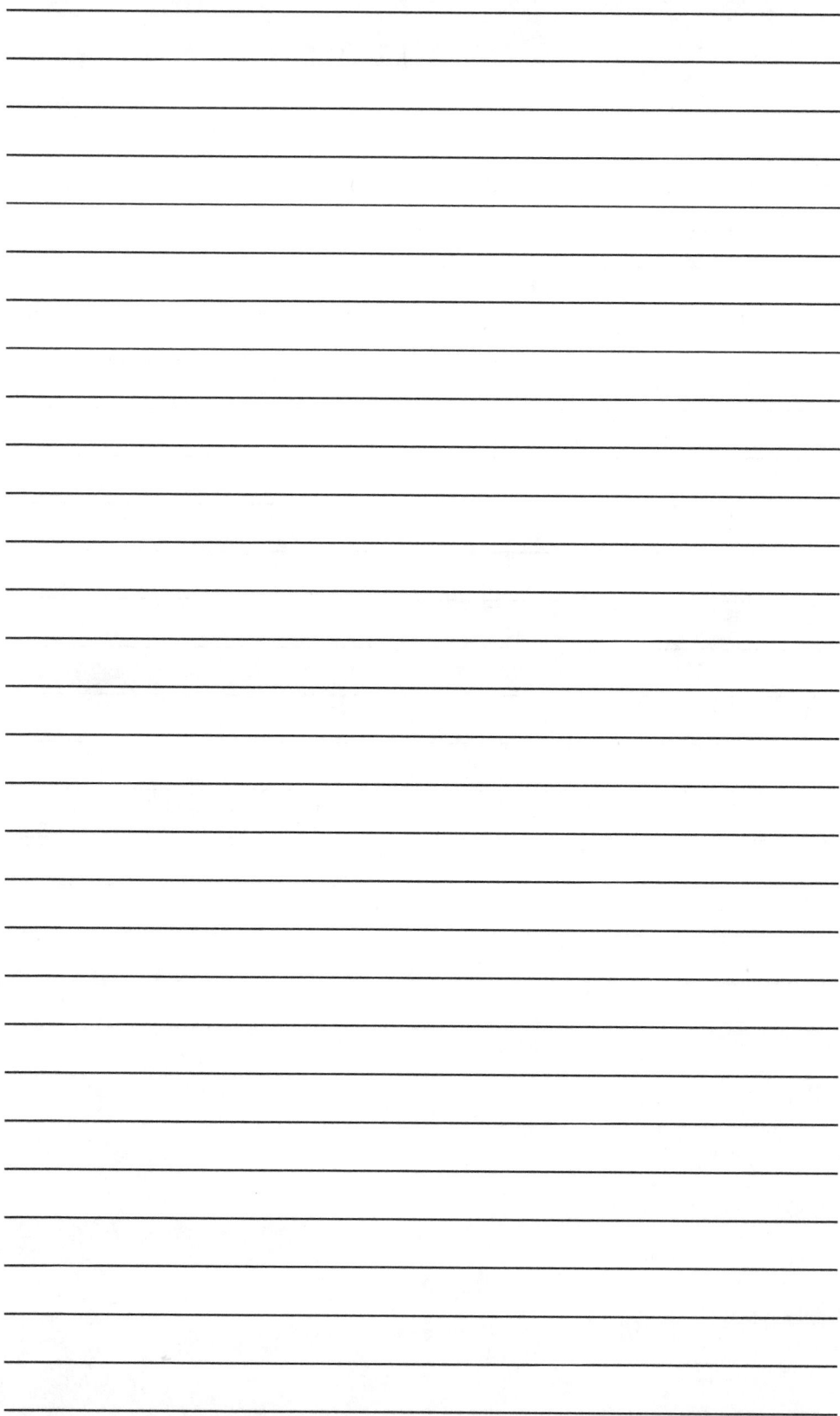

Teaching

Date_____   Speaker_____

Bible Verse _____

Topic _____

_____
_____
_____
_____
_____
_____
_____
_____
_____
_____
_____
_____
_____
_____
_____
_____
_____
_____
_____
_____
_____
_____
_____
_____
_____
_____
_____

Date: _____

Memory Verse For The Week

_____

_____

_____

_____

My Thoughts Regarding This Verse

_____

_____

_____

_____

_____

_____

_____

_____

_____

_____

_____

_____

_____

_____

_____

_____

_____

_____

Today I Am Grateful For:

_____
_____
_____
_____
_____

Daily Reading

_____
_____
_____
_____
_____
_____
_____
_____

Today's Prayer
Man ought always to pray

_____
_____
_____
_____
_____
_____
_____
_____
_____
_____

Today I Am Grateful For:

_____
_____
_____
_____
_____

Daily Reading

_____
_____
_____
_____
_____
_____
_____

Today's Prayer
Man ought always to pray

_____
_____
_____
_____
_____
_____
_____
_____
_____

Today I Am Grateful For:

_____
_____
_____
_____
_____

Daily Reading

_____
_____
_____
_____
_____
_____
_____
_____

Today's Prayer
Man ought always to pray

_____
_____
_____
_____
_____
_____
_____
_____
_____
_____

Today I Am Grateful For:

_____

_____

_____

_____

_____

Daily Reading

_____

_____

_____

_____

_____

_____

_____

_____

Today's Prayer
Man ought always to pray

_____

_____

_____

_____

_____

_____

_____

_____

_____

Today I Am Grateful For:

_____
_____
_____
_____
_____

Daily Reading

_____
_____
_____
_____
_____
_____
_____

Today's Prayer
Man ought always to pray

_____
_____
_____
_____
_____
_____
_____
_____
_____
_____

Today I Am Grateful For:

_____

_____

_____

_____

_____

Daily Reading

_____

_____

_____

_____

_____

_____

_____

Today's Prayer
Man ought always to pray

_____

_____

_____

_____

_____

_____

_____

_____

Today I Am Grateful For:

_____

_____

_____

_____

_____

Daily Reading

_____

_____

_____

_____

_____

_____

_____

Today's Prayer
Man ought always to pray

_____

_____

_____

_____

_____

_____

_____

_____

Teaching

Date_____   Speaker_____

Bible Verse _____

Topic _____

_____
_____
_____
_____
_____
_____
_____
_____
_____
_____
_____
_____
_____
_____
_____
_____
_____
_____
_____
_____
_____
_____
_____
_____
_____
_____
_____
_____
_____
_____

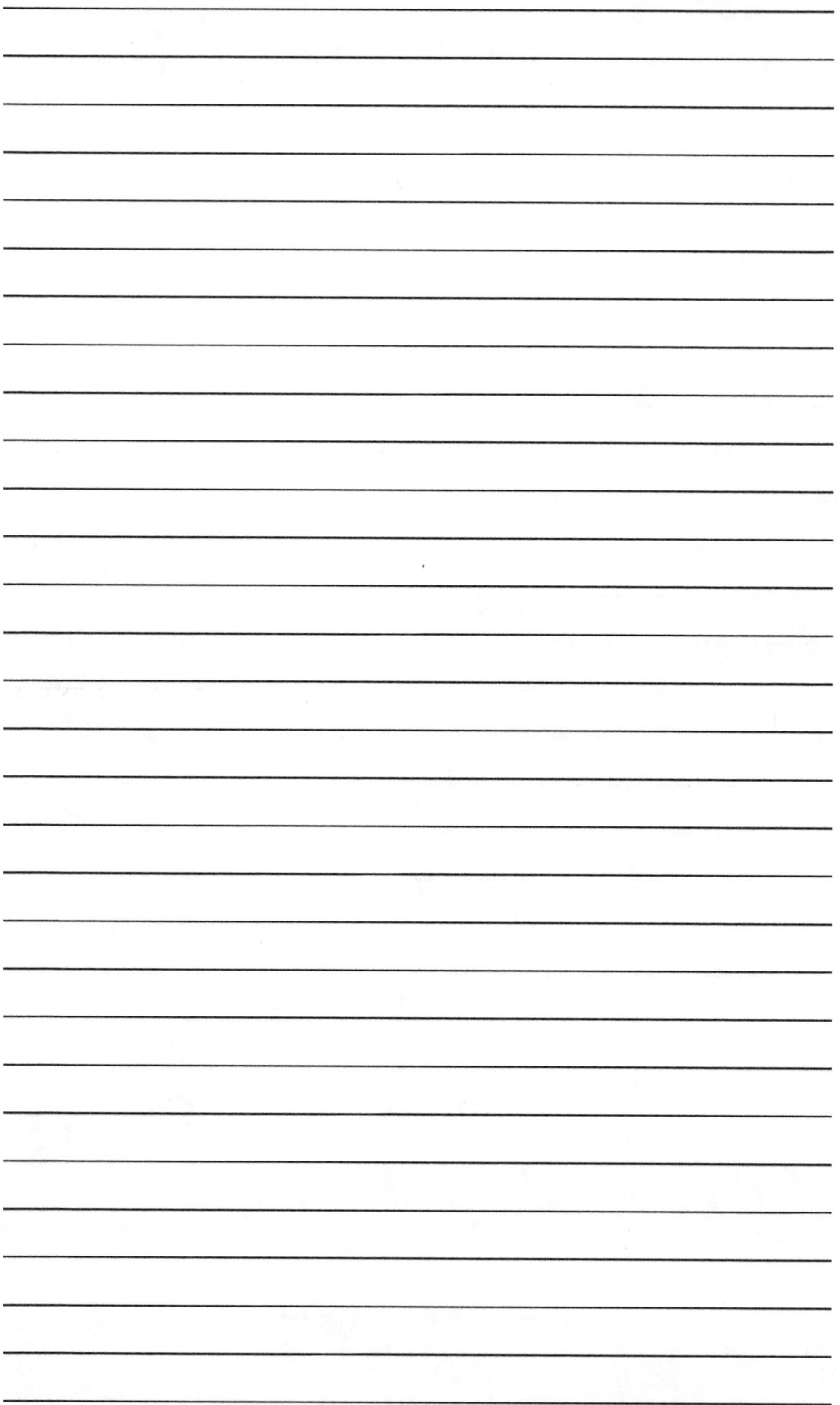

Teaching

Date_____   Speaker_____

Bible Verse _____

Topic _____

_____
_____
_____
_____
_____
_____
_____
_____
_____
_____
_____
_____
_____
_____
_____
_____
_____
_____
_____
_____
_____
_____
_____
_____
_____
_____
_____
_____
_____

Teaching

Date_____   Speaker_____

Bible Verse _____

Topic _____

_____

_____

_____

_____

_____

_____

_____

_____

_____

_____

_____

_____

_____

_____

_____

_____

_____

_____

_____

_____

_____

_____

_____

_____

_____

_____

Date: _____

Memory Verse For The Week

_____

_____

_____

_____

My Thoughts Regarding This Verse

_____

_____

_____

_____

_____

_____

_____

_____

_____

_____

_____

_____

_____

_____

_____

_____

_____

_____

_____

_____

Today I Am Grateful For:

_____
_____
_____
_____
_____

Daily Reading

_____
_____
_____
_____
_____
_____
_____
_____

Today's Prayer

Man ought always to pray

_____
_____
_____
_____
_____
_____
_____
_____
_____

Today I Am Grateful For:

_____
_____
_____
_____
_____

Daily Reading

_____
_____
_____
_____
_____
_____
_____
_____

Today's Prayer
Man ought always to pray

_____
_____
_____
_____
_____
_____
_____
_____
_____

Today I Am Grateful For:

_____
_____
_____
_____
_____

Daily Reading

_____
_____
_____
_____
_____
_____
_____
_____

Today's Prayer
Man ought always to pray

_____
_____
_____
_____
_____
_____
_____
_____
_____
_____

Today I Am Grateful For:

_____
_____
_____
_____
_____

Daily Reading

_____
_____
_____
_____
_____
_____

Today's Prayer
Man ought always to pray

_____
_____
_____
_____
_____
_____
_____
_____

Today I Am Grateful For:

_____
_____
_____
_____
_____

Daily Reading

_____
_____
_____
_____
_____
_____
_____
_____

Today's Prayer
Man ought always to pray

_____
_____
_____
_____
_____
_____
_____
_____
_____
_____
_____

Today I Am Grateful For:

_____
_____
_____
_____
_____

Daily Reading

_____
_____
_____
_____
_____
_____
_____
_____

Today's Prayer
Man ought always to pray

_____
_____
_____
_____
_____
_____
_____
_____
_____
_____

Today I Am Grateful For:

_____
_____
_____
_____
_____

Daily Reading

_____
_____
_____
_____
_____
_____
_____
_____
_____

Today's Prayer
Man ought always to pray

_____
_____
_____
_____
_____
_____
_____
_____
_____
_____

Teaching

Date_____   Speaker_____

Bible Verse _____

Topic _____

_____
_____
_____
_____
_____
_____
_____
_____
_____
_____
_____
_____
_____
_____
_____
_____
_____
_____
_____
_____
_____
_____
_____
_____
_____
_____
_____
_____

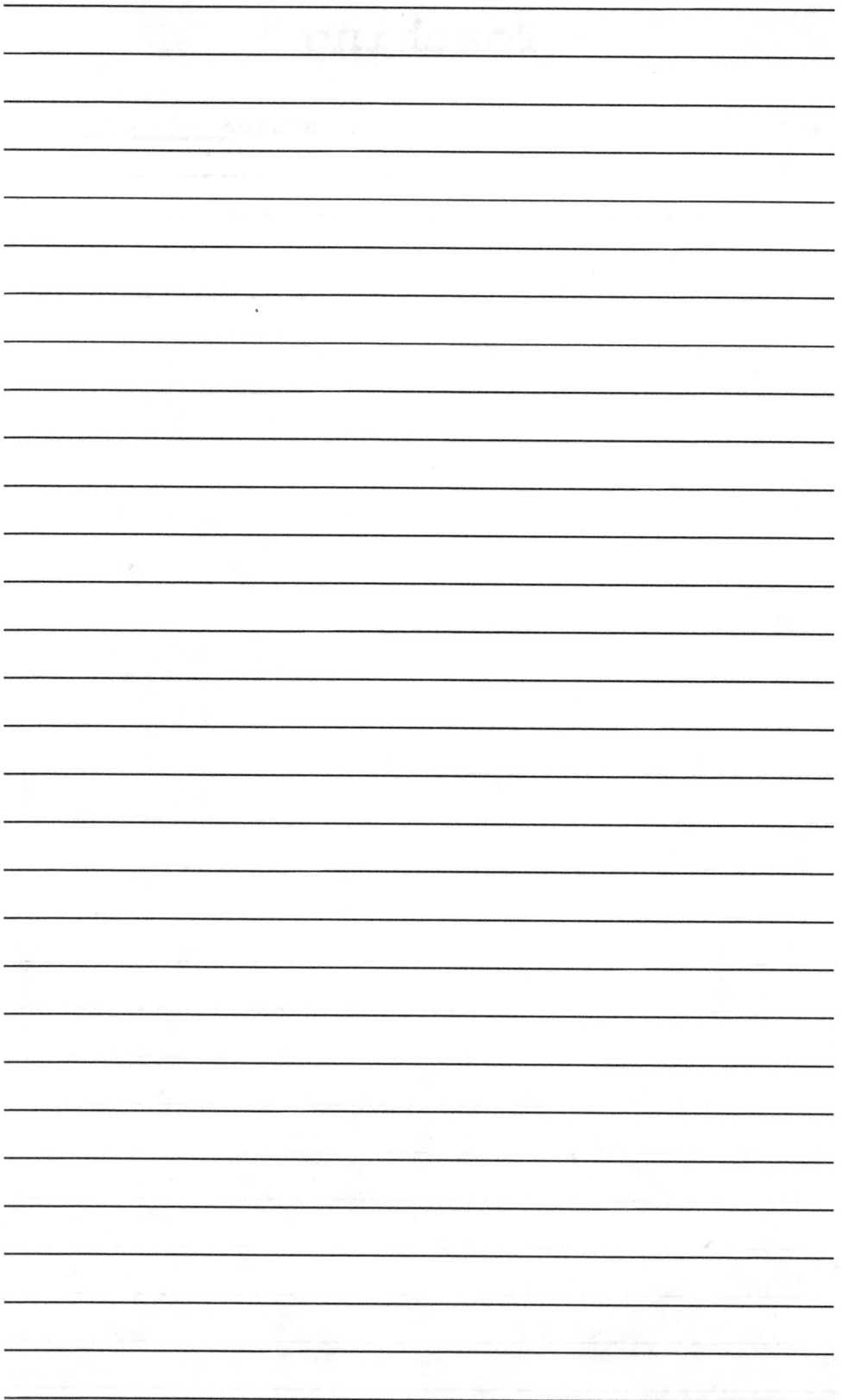

Teaching

Date_____   Speaker_____

Bible Verse _____

Topic _____

_____

_____

_____

_____

_____

_____

_____

_____

_____

_____

_____

_____

_____

_____

_____

_____

_____

_____

_____

_____

_____

_____

_____

_____

_____

_____

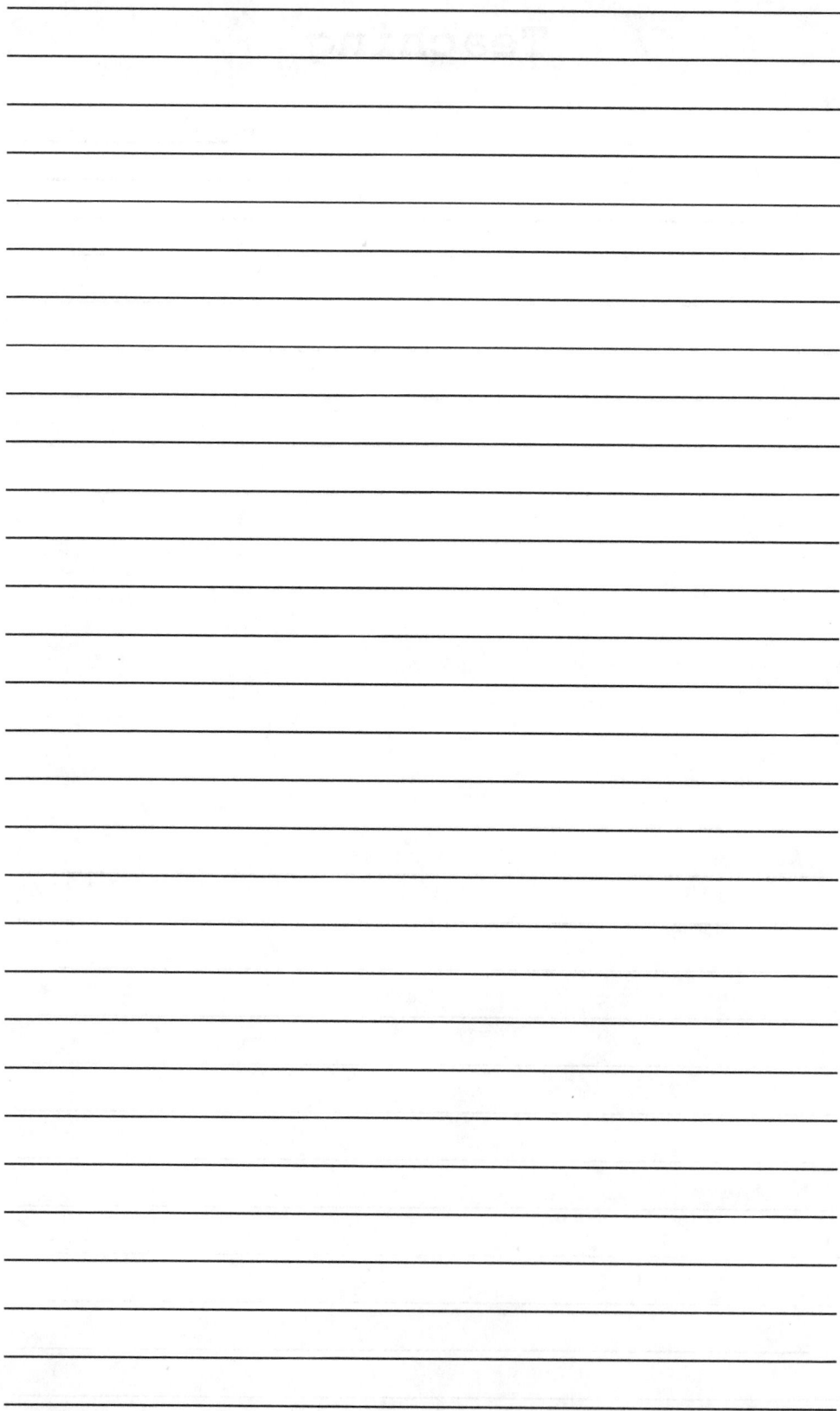

Teaching

Date_____   Speaker_____

Bible Verse _____

Topic _____

_____
_____
_____
_____
_____
_____
_____
_____
_____
_____
_____
_____
_____
_____
_____
_____
_____
_____
_____
_____
_____
_____
_____
_____
_____
_____
_____

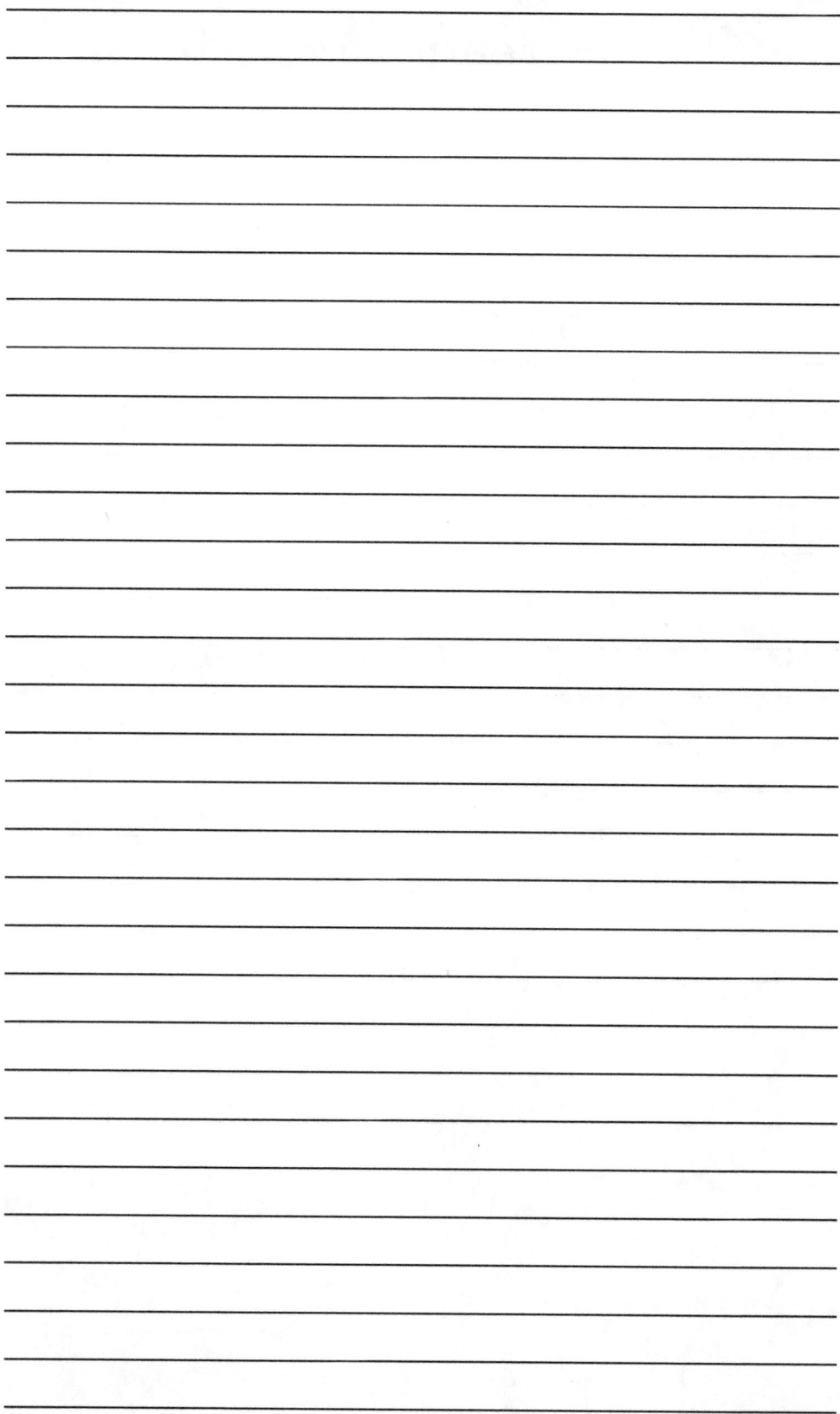

Date: _____

Memory Verse For The Week

_____

_____

_____

_____

My Thoughts Regarding This Verse

_____

_____

_____

_____

_____

_____

_____

_____

_____

_____

_____

_____

_____

_____

_____

_____

_____

_____

_____

Today I Am Grateful For:

_____
_____
_____
_____
_____

Daily Reading

_____
_____
_____
_____
_____
_____
_____
_____

Today's Prayer
Man ought always to pray

_____
_____
_____
_____
_____
_____
_____
_____
_____

Today I Am Grateful For:

_____
_____
_____
_____
_____

Daily Reading

_____
_____
_____
_____
_____
_____
_____

Today's Prayer
Man ought always to pray

_____
_____
_____
_____
_____
_____
_____
_____
_____

Today I Am Grateful For:

_____
_____
_____
_____
_____

Daily Reading

_____
_____
_____
_____
_____
_____
_____

Today's Prayer
Man ought always to pray

_____
_____
_____
_____
_____
_____
_____
_____
_____
_____

Today I Am Grateful For:

_____
_____
_____
_____
_____

Daily Reading

_____
_____
_____
_____
_____
_____
_____

Today's Prayer
Man ought always to pray

_____
_____
_____
_____
_____
_____
_____
_____
_____

Today I Am Grateful For:

_____

_____

_____

_____

_____

Daily Reading

_____

_____

_____

_____

_____

_____

_____

_____

Today's Prayer
Man ought always to pray

_____

_____

_____

_____

_____

_____

_____

_____

_____

Today I Am Grateful For:

_____

_____

_____

_____

_____

Daily Reading

_____

_____

_____

_____

_____

_____

Today's Prayer
Man ought always to pray

_____

_____

_____

_____

_____

_____

_____

_____

Today I Am Grateful For:

_____

_____

_____

_____

Daily Reading

_____

_____

_____

_____

_____

_____

_____

Today's Prayer
Man ought always to pray

_____

_____

_____

_____

_____

_____

_____

_____

_____

Teaching

Date_____   Speaker_____

Bible Verse _____

Topic _____

_____

_____

_____

_____

_____

_____

_____

_____

_____

_____

_____

_____

_____

_____

_____

_____

_____

_____

_____

_____

_____

_____

_____

_____

_____

_____

_____

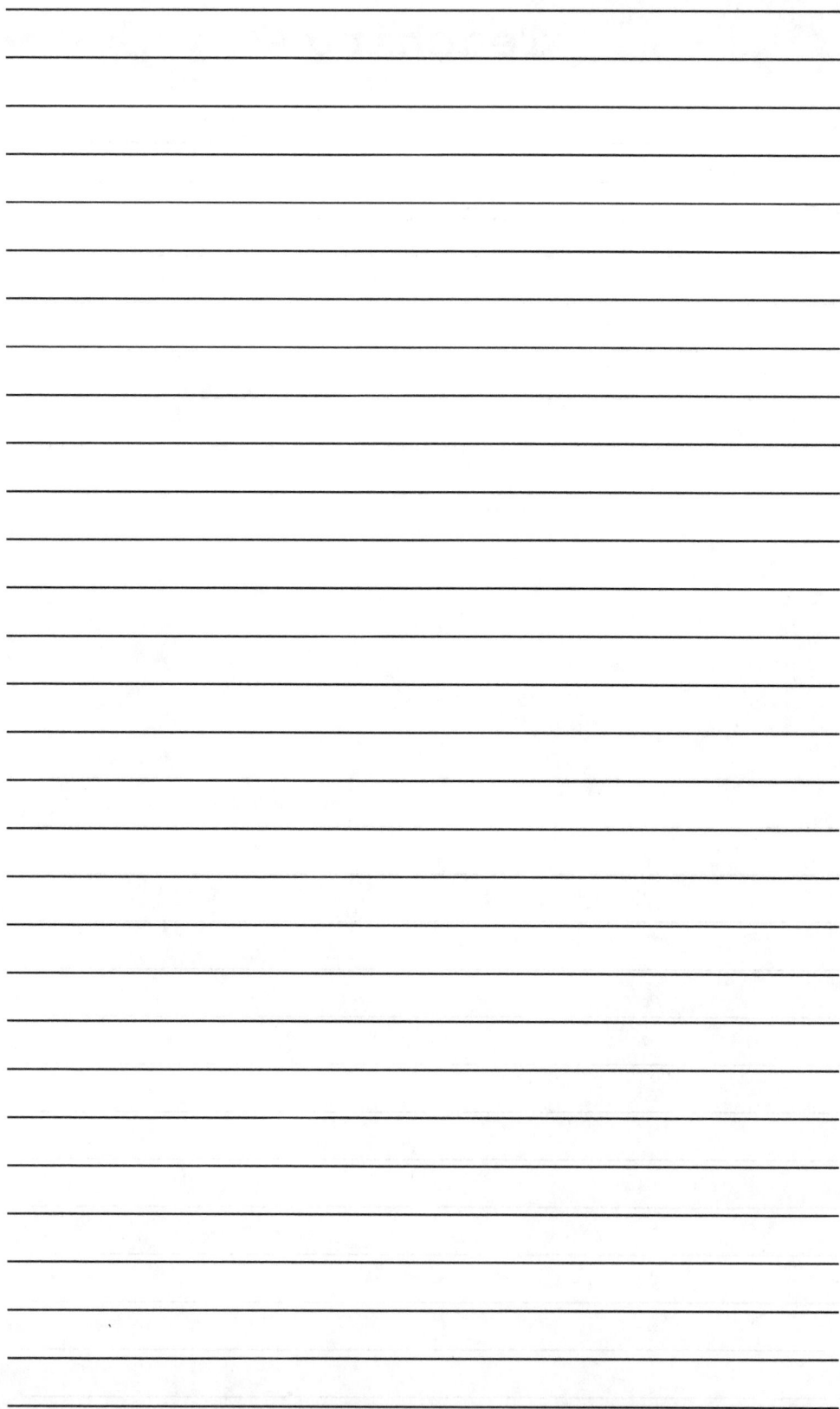

Teaching

Date_____   Speaker_____

Bible Verse _____

Topic _____

_____

_____

_____

_____

_____

_____

_____

_____

_____

_____

_____

_____

_____

_____

_____

_____

_____

_____

_____

_____

_____

_____

_____

_____

_____

_____

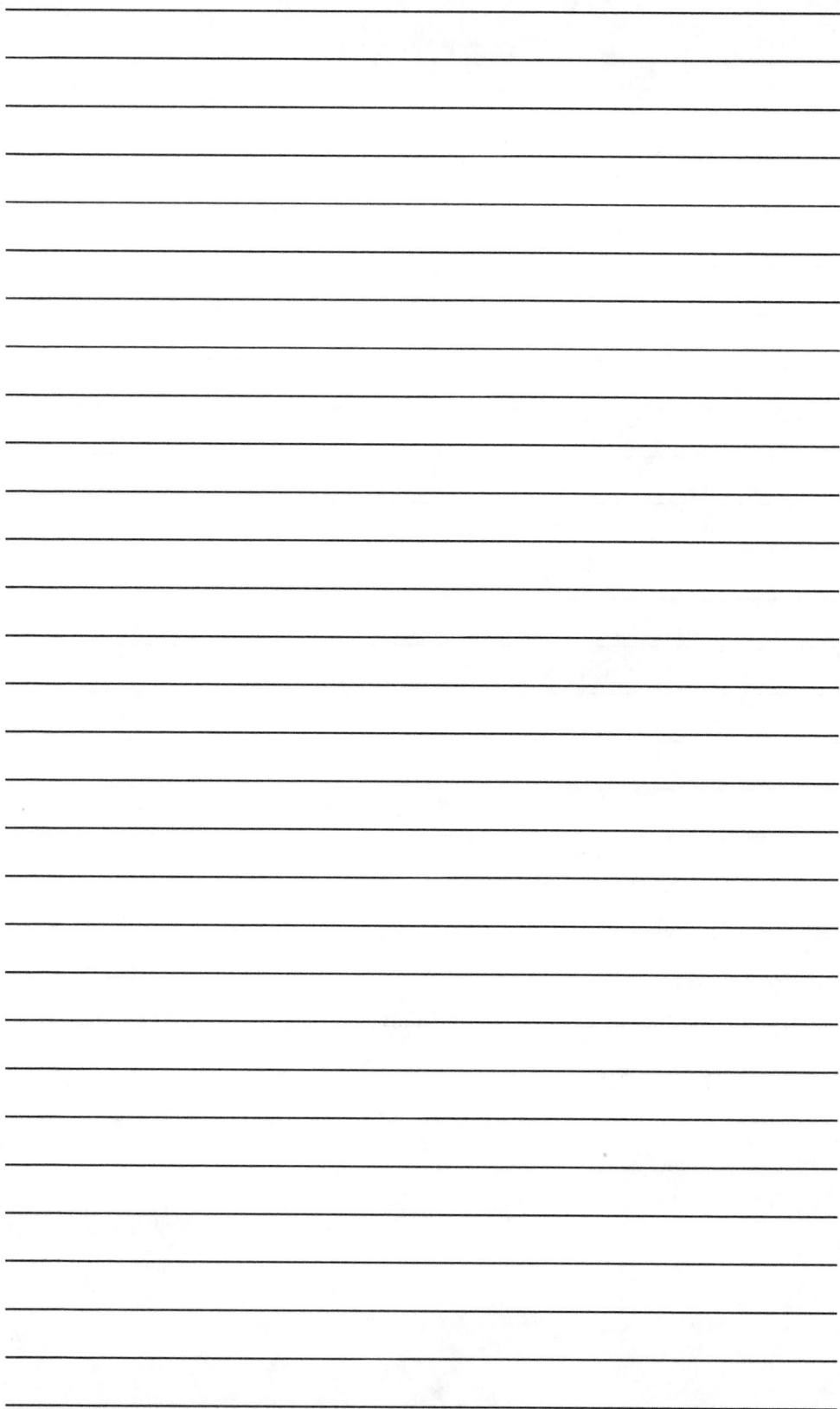

Teaching

Date_____   Speaker_____

Bible Verse _____

Topic _____

_____
_____
_____
_____
_____
_____
_____
_____
_____
_____
_____
_____
_____
_____
_____
_____
_____
_____
_____
_____
_____
_____
_____
_____
_____
_____
_____

Date: _____

Memory Verse For The Week

_____

_____

_____

_____

My Thoughts Regarding This Verse

_____

_____

_____

_____

_____

_____

_____

_____

_____

_____

_____

_____

_____

_____

_____

_____

_____

_____

_____

Today I Am Grateful For:

_____
_____
_____
_____
_____

Daily Reading

_____
_____
_____
_____
_____
_____
_____

Today's Prayer
Man ought always to pray

_____
_____
_____
_____
_____
_____
_____
_____
_____
_____

Today I Am Grateful For:

_____

_____

_____

_____

_____

Daily Reading

_____

_____

_____

_____

_____

_____

_____

Today's Prayer
Man ought always to pray

_____

_____

_____

_____

_____

_____

_____

_____

_____

Today I Am Grateful For:

_____

_____

_____

_____

_____

Daily Reading

_____

_____

_____

_____

_____

_____

_____

Today's Prayer
Man ought always to pray

_____

_____

_____

_____

_____

_____

_____

_____

_____

Today I Am Grateful For:

_____

_____

_____

_____

_____

Daily Reading

_____

_____

_____

_____

_____

_____

Today's Prayer
Man ought always to pray

_____

_____

_____

_____

_____

_____

_____

_____

Today I Am Grateful For:

_____
_____
_____
_____
_____

Daily Reading

_____
_____
_____
_____
_____
_____
_____

Today's Prayer
Man ought always to pray

_____
_____
_____
_____
_____
_____
_____
_____
_____
_____

Today I Am Grateful For:

_____

_____

_____

_____

_____

Daily Reading

_____

_____

_____

_____

_____

_____

_____

Today's Prayer
Man ought always to pray

_____

_____

_____

_____

_____

_____

_____

_____

_____

Today I Am Grateful For:

_____

_____

_____

_____

_____

Daily Reading

_____

_____

_____

_____

_____

_____

_____

Today's Prayer
Man ought always to pray

_____

_____

_____

_____

_____

_____

_____

_____

_____

Teaching

Date_____   Speaker_____

Bible Verse _____

Topic _____

_____

_____

_____

_____

_____

_____

_____

_____

_____

_____

_____

_____

_____

_____

_____

_____

_____

_____

_____

_____

_____

_____

_____

_____

_____

_____

_____

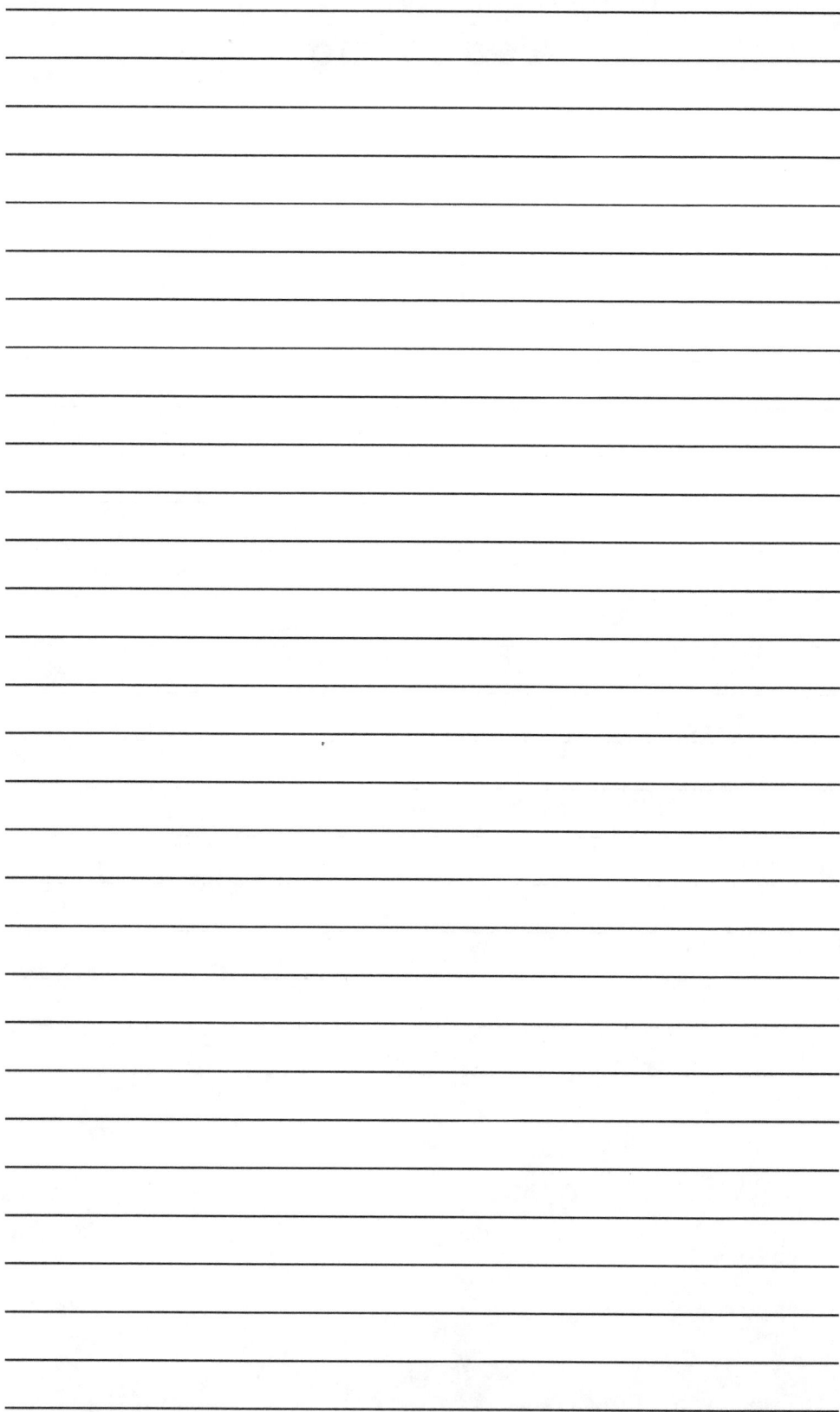

Teaching

Date_____   Speaker_____

Bible Verse _____

Topic _____

_____
_____
_____
_____
_____
_____
_____
_____
_____
_____
_____
_____
_____
_____
_____
_____
_____
_____
_____
_____
_____
_____
_____
_____
_____
_____
_____
_____

Teaching

Date_____   Speaker_____

Bible Verse _____

Topic _____

_____

_____

_____

_____

_____

_____

_____

_____

_____

_____

_____

_____

_____

_____

_____

_____

_____

_____

_____

_____

_____

_____

_____

_____

_____

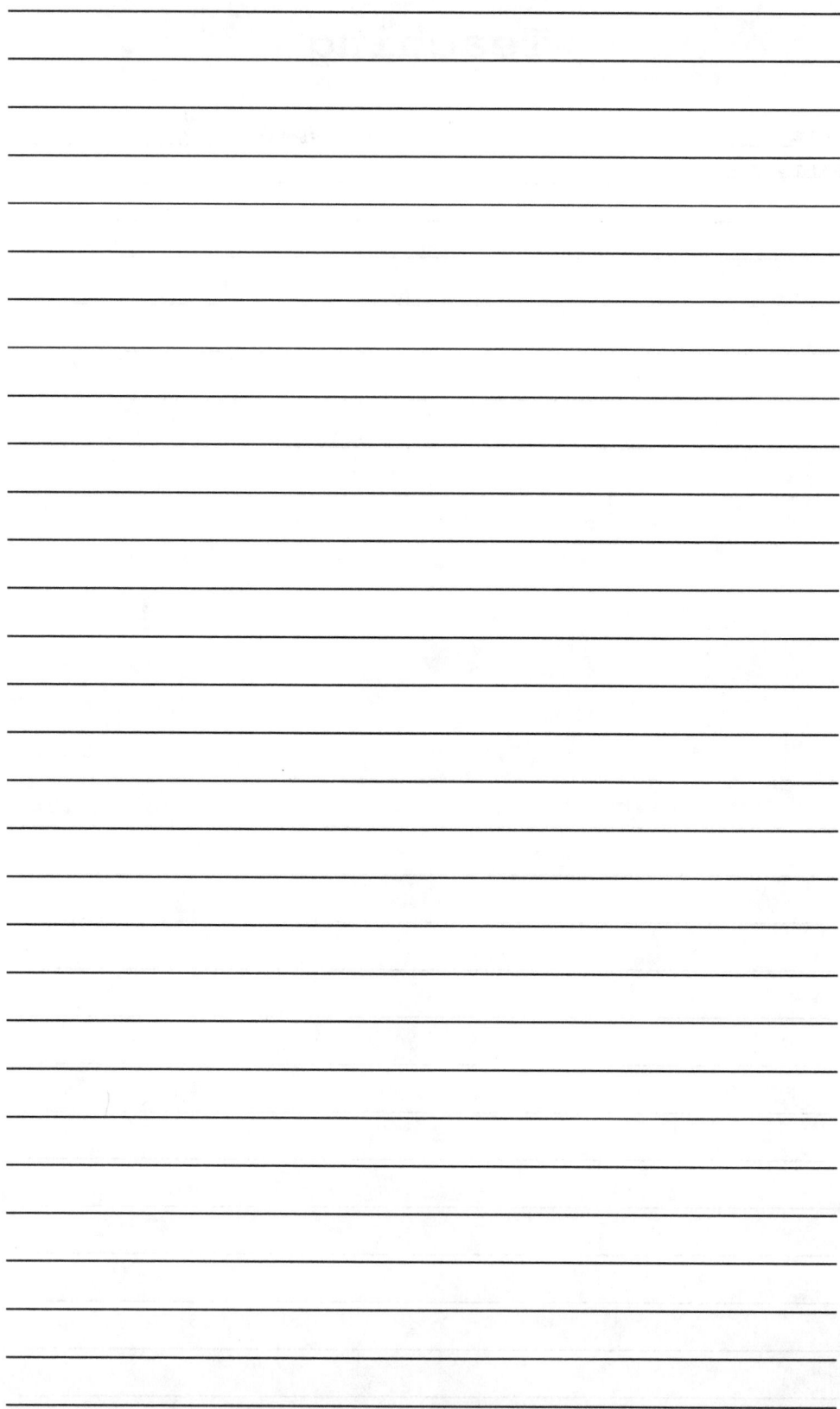

Date: _____

Memory Verse For The Week

_____

_____

_____

_____

My Thoughts Regarding This Verse

_____

_____

_____

_____

_____

_____

_____

_____

_____

_____

_____

_____

_____

_____

_____

_____

_____

_____

_____

_____

Today I Am Grateful For:

_____

_____

_____

_____

_____

Daily Reading

_____

_____

_____

_____

_____

_____

_____

Today's Prayer
Man ought always to pray

_____

_____

_____

_____

_____

_____

_____

_____

Today I Am Grateful For:

_____
_____
_____
_____
_____

Daily Reading

_____
_____
_____
_____
_____
_____
_____

Today's Prayer
Man ought always to pray

_____
_____
_____
_____
_____
_____
_____
_____
_____

Today I Am Grateful For:

_____
_____
_____
_____
_____

Daily Reading

_____
_____
_____
_____
_____
_____
_____
_____

Today's Prayer
Man ought always to pray

_____
_____
_____
_____
_____
_____
_____
_____
_____
_____

Today I Am Grateful For:

_____
_____
_____
_____
_____

Daily Reading

_____
_____
_____
_____
_____
_____
_____

Today's Prayer
Man ought always to pray

_____
_____
_____
_____
_____
_____
_____
_____

Today I Am Grateful For:

_____
_____
_____
_____
_____

Daily Reading

_____
_____
_____
_____
_____
_____
_____
_____

Today's Prayer
Man ought always to pray

_____
_____
_____
_____
_____
_____
_____
_____
_____
_____

Today I Am Grateful For:

_____

_____

_____

_____

_____

Daily Reading

_____

_____

_____

_____

_____

_____

_____

Today's Prayer
Man ought always to pray

_____

_____

_____

_____

_____

_____

_____

_____

_____

Today I Am Grateful For:

_____
_____
_____
_____
_____

Daily Reading

_____
_____
_____
_____
_____
_____
_____
_____

Today's Prayer
Man ought always to pray

_____
_____
_____
_____
_____
_____
_____
_____
_____
_____

Teaching

Date_____   Speaker_____

Bible Verse _____

Topic _____

_____
_____
_____
_____
_____
_____
_____
_____
_____
_____
_____
_____
_____
_____
_____
_____
_____
_____
_____
_____
_____
_____
_____
_____
_____
_____
_____
_____

Teaching

Date_____   Speaker_____

Bible Verse _____

Topic _____

_____
_____
_____
_____
_____
_____
_____
_____
_____
_____
_____
_____
_____
_____
_____
_____
_____
_____
_____
_____
_____
_____
_____
_____
_____
_____
_____
_____

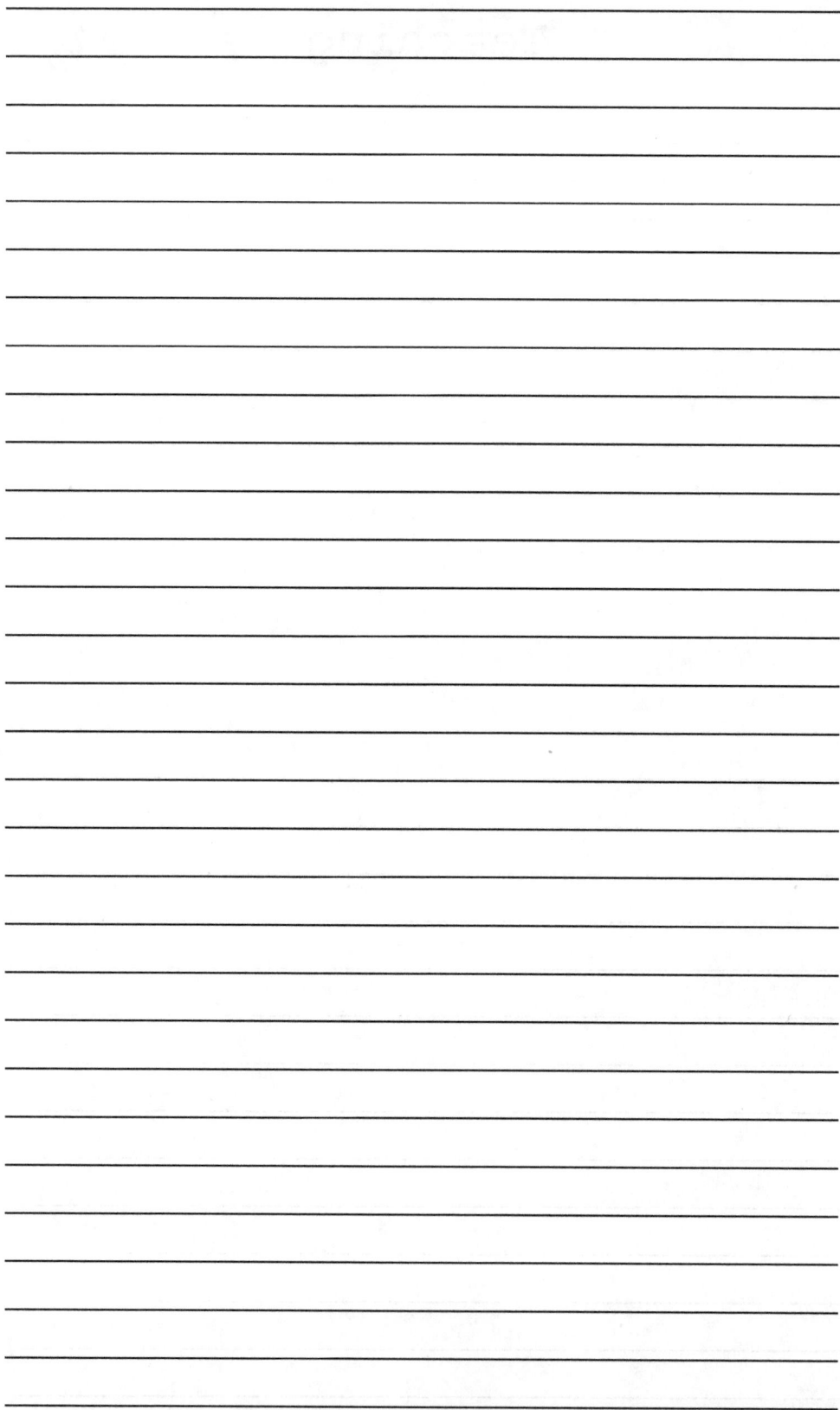

Teaching

Date_____   Speaker_____

Bible Verse _____

Topic _____

_____

_____

_____

_____

_____

_____

_____

_____

_____

_____

_____

_____

_____

_____

_____

_____

_____

_____

_____

_____

_____

_____

_____

_____

_____

_____

_____

_____

_____

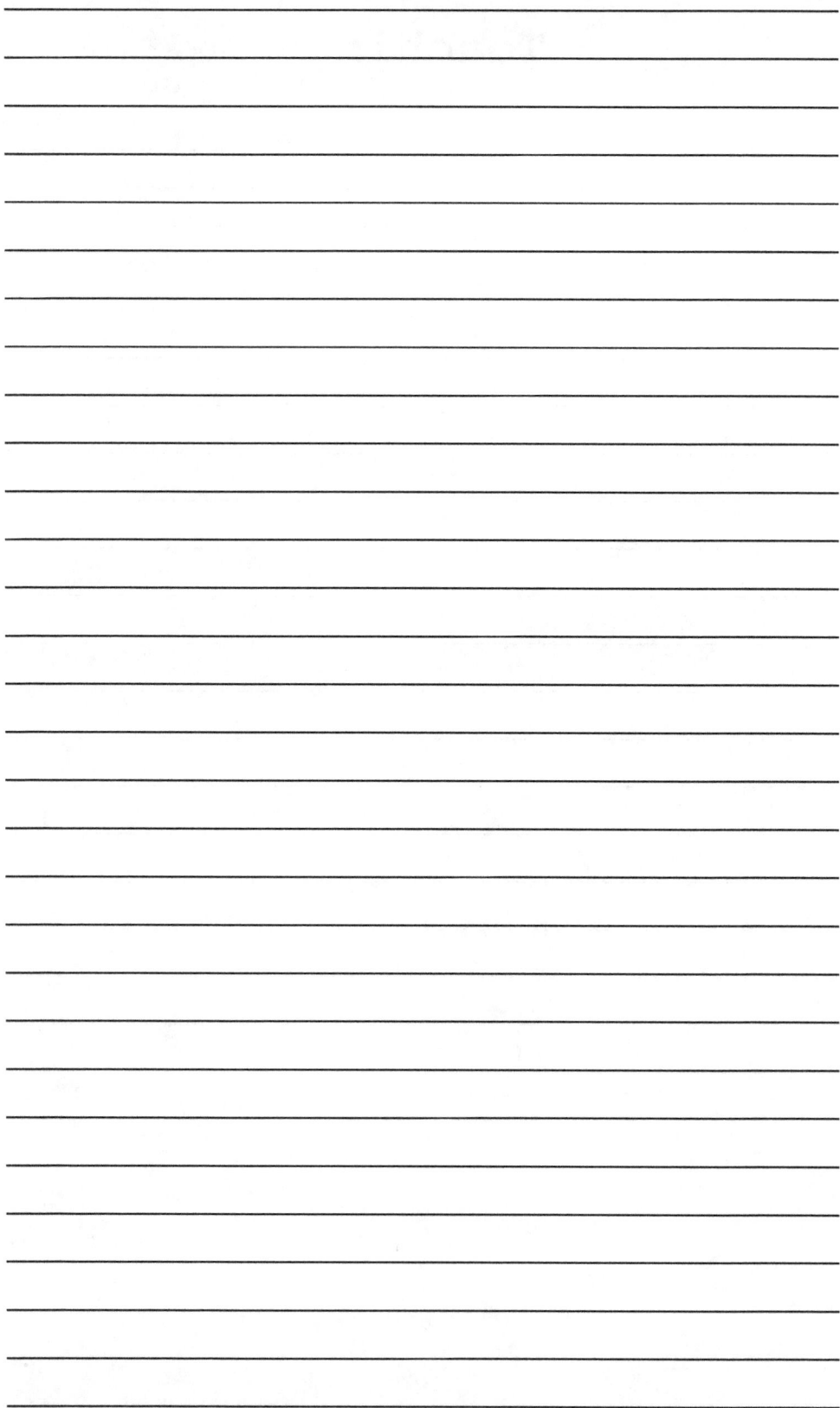

Date: _____

Memory Verse For The Week

_____

_____

_____

_____

My Thoughts Regarding This Verse

_____

_____

_____

_____

_____

_____

_____

_____

_____

_____

_____

_____

_____

_____

_____

_____

_____

_____

Today I Am Grateful For:

_____
_____
_____
_____
_____

Daily Reading

_____
_____
_____
_____
_____
_____
_____
_____

Today's Prayer
Man ought always to pray

_____
_____
_____
_____
_____
_____
_____
_____
_____
_____

Today I Am Grateful For:

Daily Reading

Today's Prayer
Man ought always to pray

Today I Am Grateful For:

_____
_____
_____
_____
_____

Daily Reading

_____
_____
_____
_____
_____
_____
_____
_____

Today's Prayer
Man ought always to pray

_____
_____
_____
_____
_____
_____
_____
_____
_____
_____

Today I Am Grateful For:

_____

_____

_____

_____

_____

Daily Reading

_____

_____

_____

_____

_____

_____

_____

Today's Prayer
Man ought always to pray

_____

_____

_____

_____

_____

_____

_____

_____

_____

Today I Am Grateful For:

_____
_____
_____
_____
_____

Daily Reading

_____
_____
_____
_____
_____
_____
_____
_____

Today's Prayer
Man ought always to pray

_____
_____
_____
_____
_____
_____
_____
_____
_____
_____

Today I Am Grateful For:

_____

_____

_____

_____

_____

Daily Reading

_____

_____

_____

_____

_____

_____

Today's Prayer
Man ought always to pray

_____

_____

_____

_____

_____

_____

_____

_____

Today I Am Grateful For:

_____
_____
_____
_____
_____

Daily Reading

_____
_____
_____
_____
_____
_____
_____
_____

Today's Prayer
Man ought always to pray

_____
_____
_____
_____
_____
_____
_____
_____
_____
_____

Teaching

Date_____   Speaker_____

Bible Verse _____

Topic _____

_____

_____

_____

_____

_____

_____

_____

_____

_____

_____

_____

_____

_____

_____

_____

_____

_____

_____

_____

_____

_____

_____

_____

_____

_____

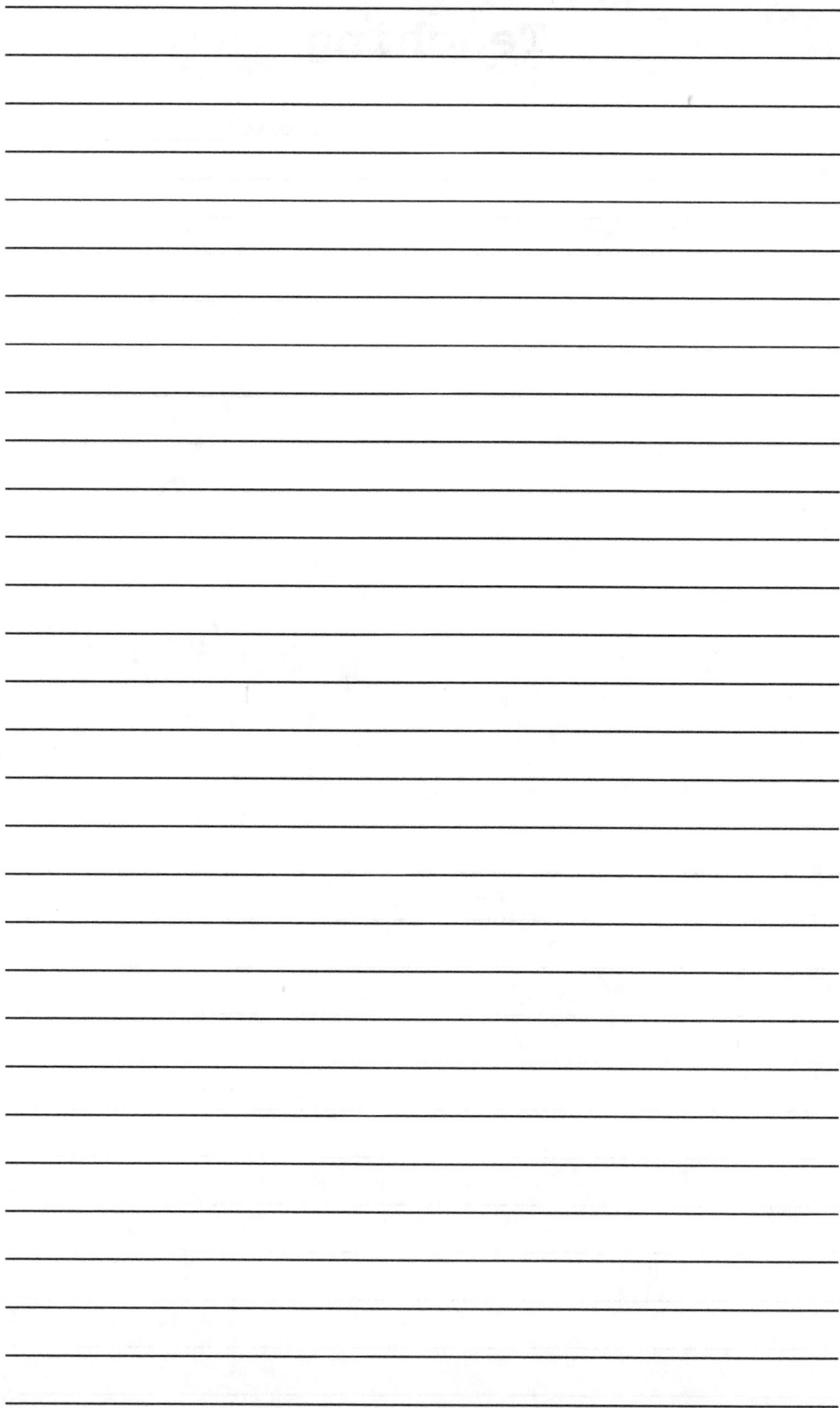

Teaching

Date_____   Speaker_____

Bible Verse _____

Topic _____

_____
_____
_____
_____
_____
_____
_____
_____
_____
_____
_____
_____
_____
_____
_____
_____
_____
_____
_____
_____
_____
_____
_____
_____
_____
_____
_____
_____
_____
_____
_____
_____

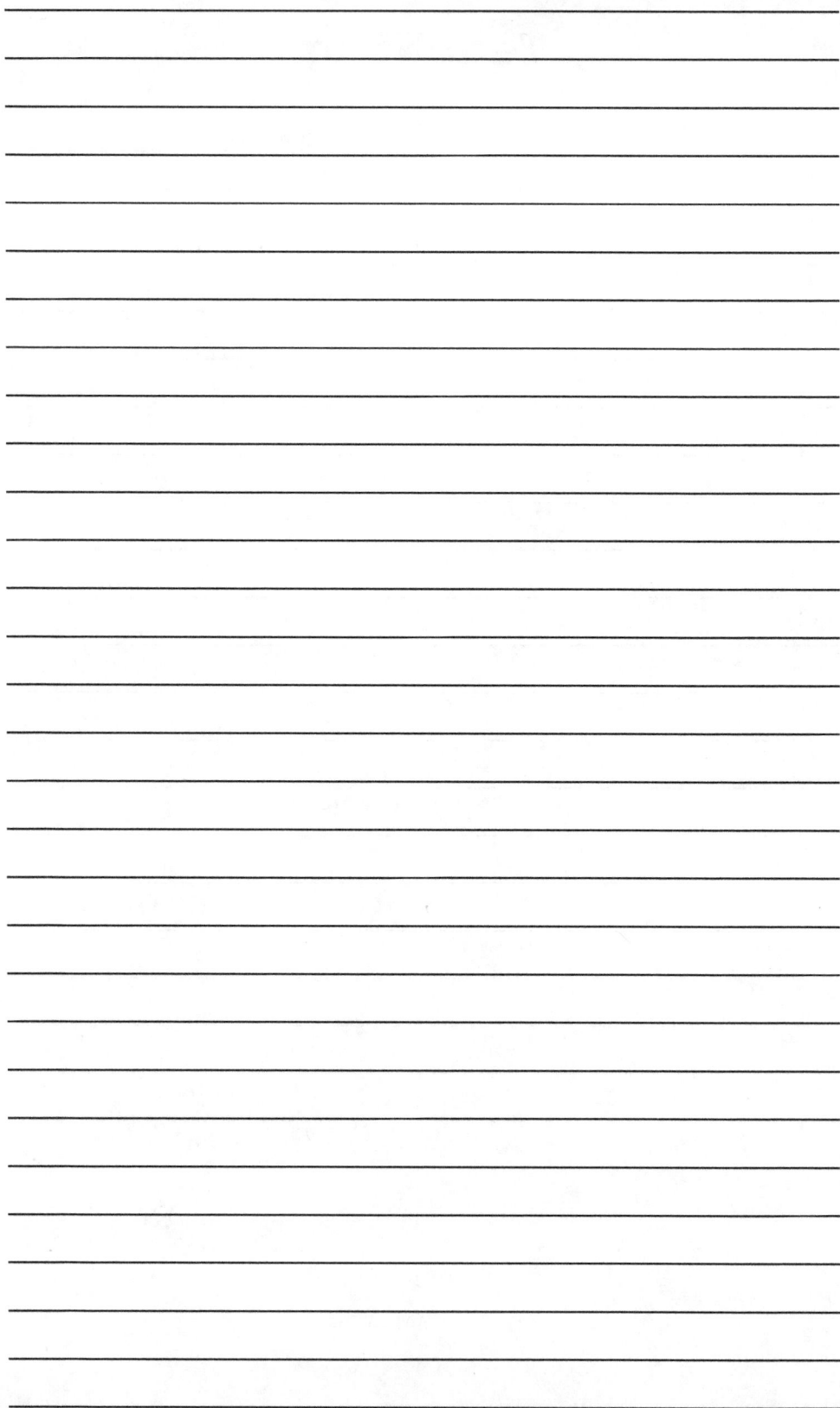

Teaching

Date_____   Speaker_____

Bible Verse _____

Topic _____

_____
_____
_____
_____
_____
_____
_____
_____
_____
_____
_____
_____
_____
_____
_____
_____
_____
_____
_____
_____
_____
_____
_____
_____
_____
_____
_____
_____
_____

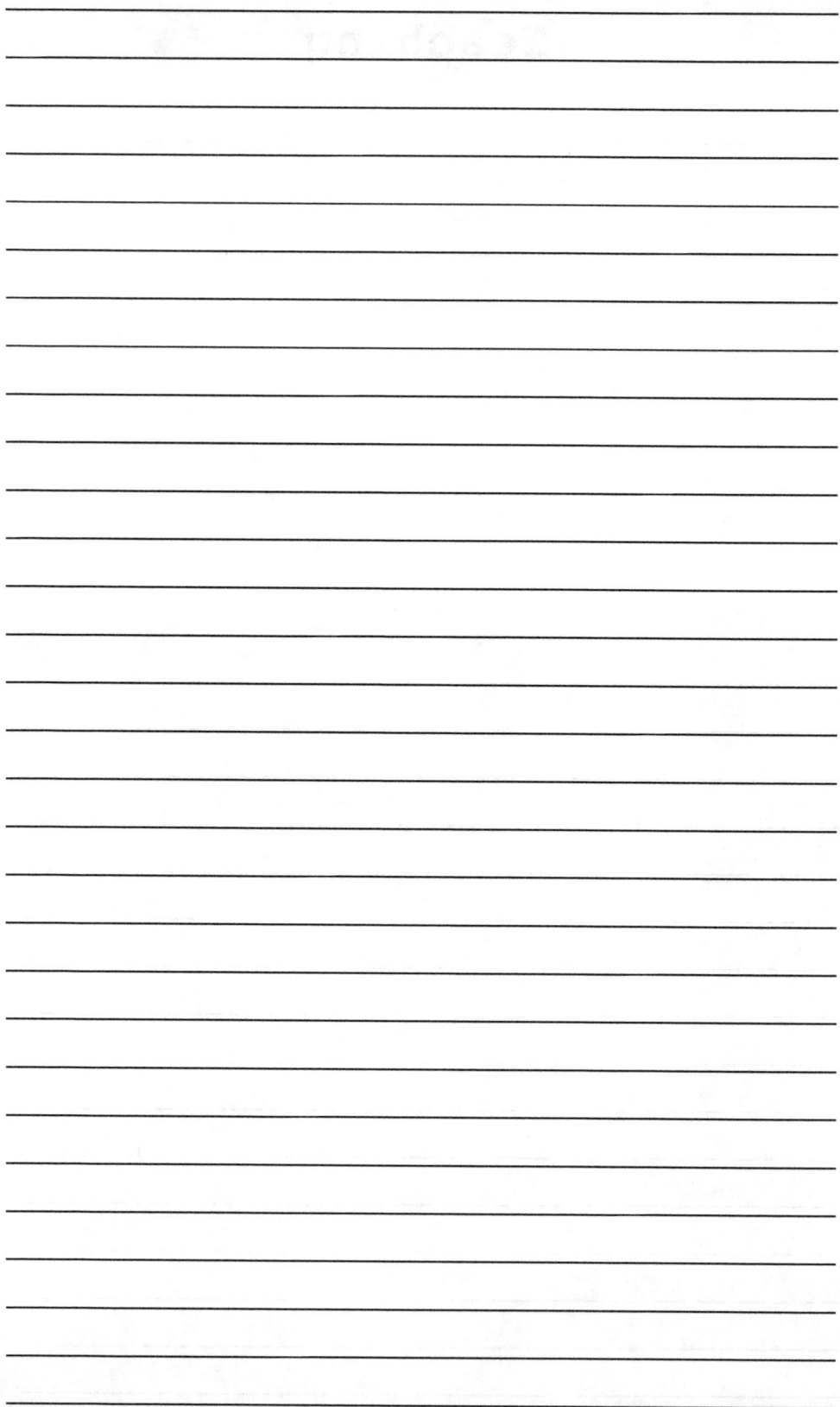

Date: _____

Memory Verse For The Week

_____

_____

_____

_____

My Thoughts Regarding This Verse

_____

_____

_____

_____

_____

_____

_____

_____

_____

_____

_____

_____

_____

_____

_____

_____

_____

_____

_____

Today I Am Grateful For:

_____
_____
_____
_____
_____

Daily Reading

_____
_____
_____
_____
_____
_____
_____

Today's Prayer
Man ought always to pray

_____
_____
_____
_____
_____
_____
_____
_____
_____
_____

Today I Am Grateful For:

_____

_____

_____

_____

_____

Daily Reading

_____

_____

_____

_____

_____

_____

_____

Today's Prayer
Man ought always to pray

_____

_____

_____

_____

_____

_____

_____

_____

_____

Today I Am Grateful For:

_____
_____
_____
_____
_____

Daily Reading

_____
_____
_____
_____
_____
_____
_____
_____
_____

Today's Prayer
Man ought always to pray

_____
_____
_____
_____
_____
_____
_____
_____
_____
_____

Today I Am Grateful For:

_____

_____

_____

_____

_____

Daily Reading

_____

_____

_____

_____

_____

_____

_____

Today's Prayer
Man ought always to pray

_____

_____

_____

_____

_____

_____

_____

_____

Today I Am Grateful For:

_____
_____
_____
_____
_____

Daily Reading

_____
_____
_____
_____
_____
_____
_____
_____

Today's Prayer
Man ought always to pray

_____
_____
_____
_____
_____
_____
_____
_____
_____

Today I Am Grateful For:

_____

_____

_____

_____

_____

Daily Reading

_____

_____

_____

_____

_____

_____

_____

Today's Prayer
Man ought always to pray

_____

_____

_____

_____

_____

_____

_____

_____

_____

Today I Am Grateful For:

_____

_____

_____

_____

_____

Daily Reading

_____

_____

_____

_____

_____

_____

_____

Today's Prayer
Man ought always to pray

_____

_____

_____

_____

_____

_____

_____

_____

_____

Teaching

Date_____   Speaker_____

Bible Verse _____

Topic _____

_____
_____
_____
_____
_____
_____
_____
_____
_____
_____
_____
_____
_____
_____
_____
_____
_____
_____
_____
_____
_____
_____
_____
_____
_____
_____
_____
_____
_____

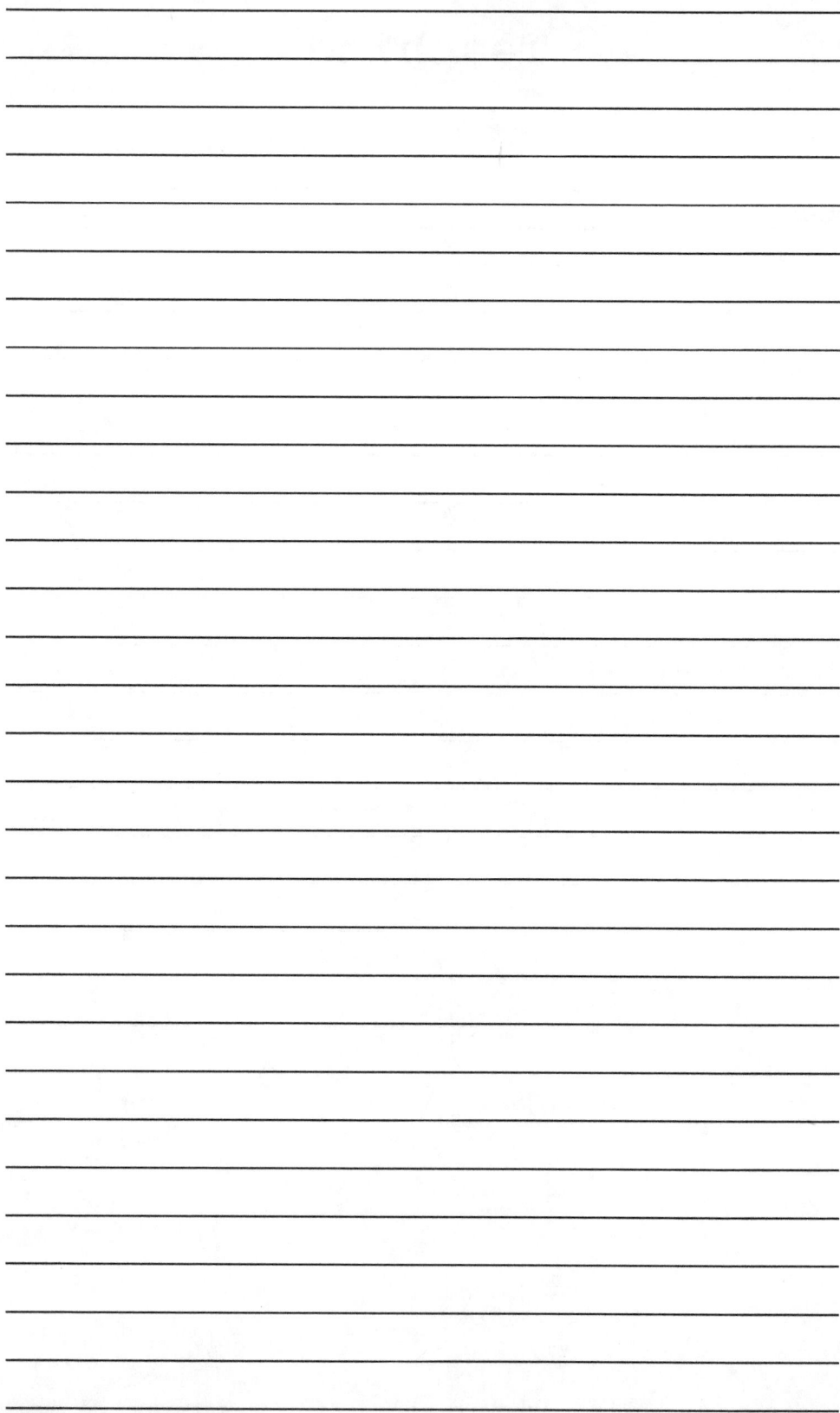

Teaching

Date_____ Speaker_____

Bible Verse _____

Topic _____

_____
_____
_____
_____
_____
_____
_____
_____
_____
_____
_____
_____
_____
_____
_____
_____
_____
_____
_____
_____
_____
_____
_____
_____
_____
_____
_____
_____

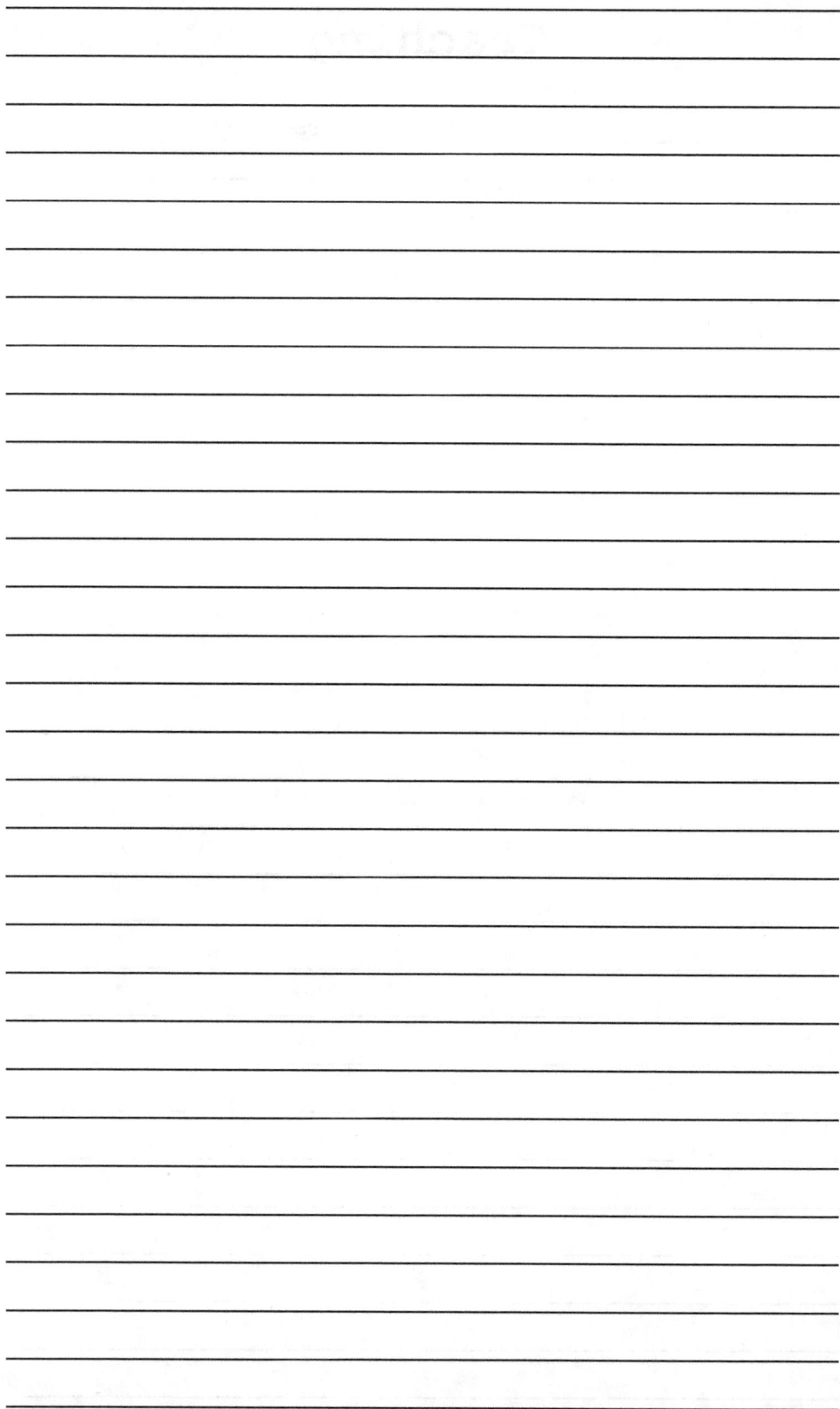

Teaching

Date_____   Speaker_____

Bible Verse _____

Topic _____

_____

_____

_____

_____

_____

_____

_____

_____

_____

_____

_____

_____

_____

_____

_____

_____

_____

_____

_____

_____

_____

_____

_____

_____

_____

_____

_____

_____

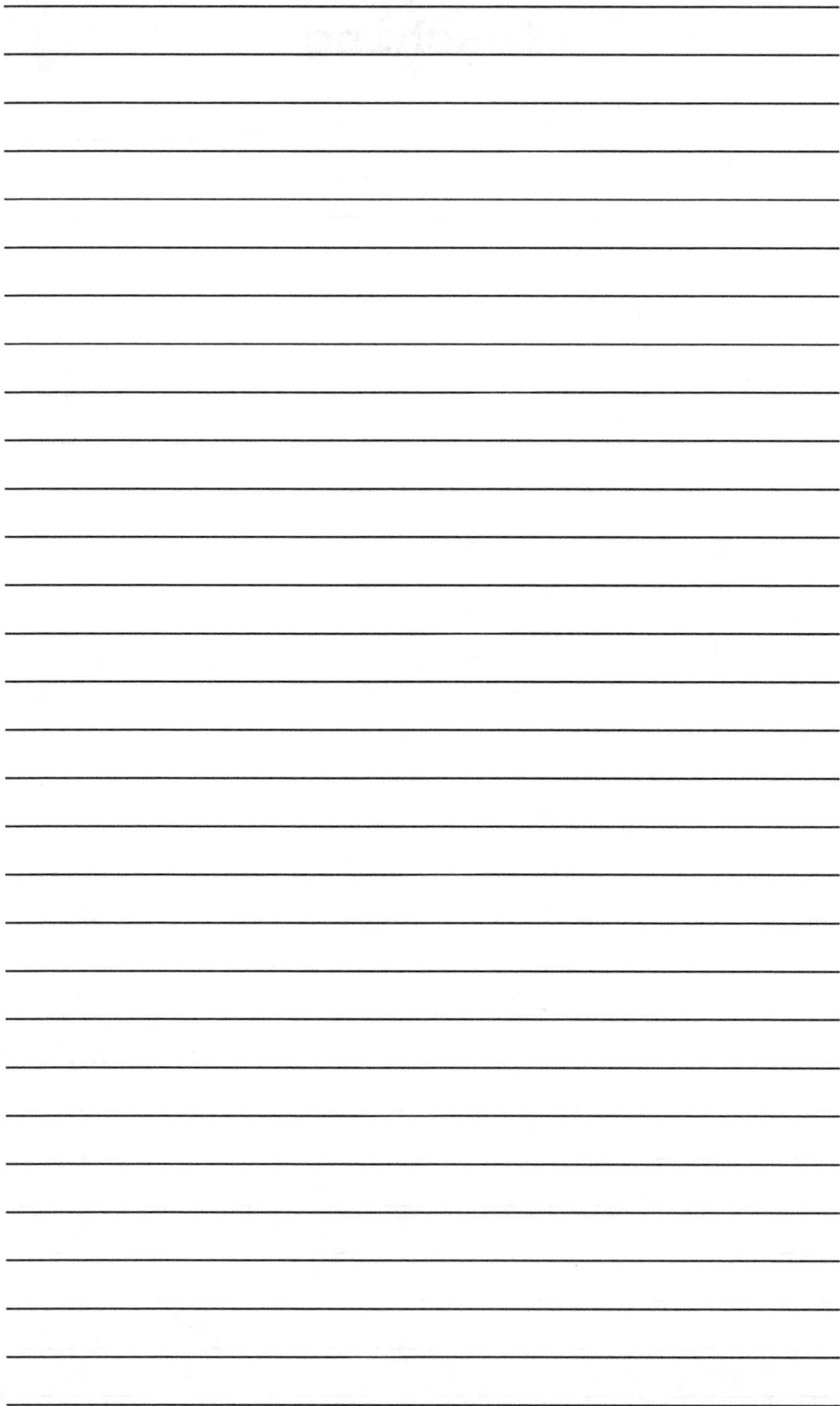

Memory Verse For The Week

_____

_____

_____

_____

My Thoughts Regarding This Verse

_____

_____

_____

_____

_____

_____

_____

_____

_____

_____

_____

_____

_____

_____

_____

_____

_____

_____

_____

Today I Am Grateful For:

_____
_____
_____
_____
_____

Daily Reading

_____
_____
_____
_____
_____
_____
_____
_____

Today's Prayer
Man ought always to pray

_____
_____
_____
_____
_____
_____
_____
_____
_____
_____

Today I Am Grateful For:

_____

_____

_____

_____

_____

Daily Reading

_____

_____

_____

_____

_____

_____

_____

Today's Prayer
Man ought always to pray

_____

_____

_____

_____

_____

_____

_____

_____

Today I Am Grateful For:

_____

_____

_____

_____

_____

Daily Reading

_____

_____

_____

_____

_____

_____

_____

Today's Prayer
Man ought always to pray

_____

_____

_____

_____

_____

_____

_____

_____

_____

_____

Today I Am Grateful For:

_____

_____

_____

_____

Daily Reading

_____

_____

_____

_____

_____

_____

Today's Prayer
Man ought always to pray

_____

_____

_____

_____

_____

_____

_____

_____

Today I Am Grateful For:

_____

_____

_____

_____

_____

Daily Reading

_____

_____

_____

_____

_____

_____

_____

Today's Prayer
Man ought always to pray

_____

_____

_____

_____

_____

_____

_____

_____

_____

Today I Am Grateful For:

_____
_____
_____
_____
_____

Daily Reading

_____
_____
_____
_____
_____
_____
_____

Today's Prayer
Man ought always to pray

_____
_____
_____
_____
_____
_____
_____
_____
_____

Today I Am Grateful For:

Daily Reading

Today's Prayer
Man ought always to pray

Teaching

Date_____   Speaker_____

Bible Verse _____

Topic _____

_____
_____
_____
_____
_____
_____
_____
_____
_____
_____
_____
_____
_____
_____
_____
_____
_____
_____
_____
_____
_____
_____
_____
_____
_____
_____
_____
_____

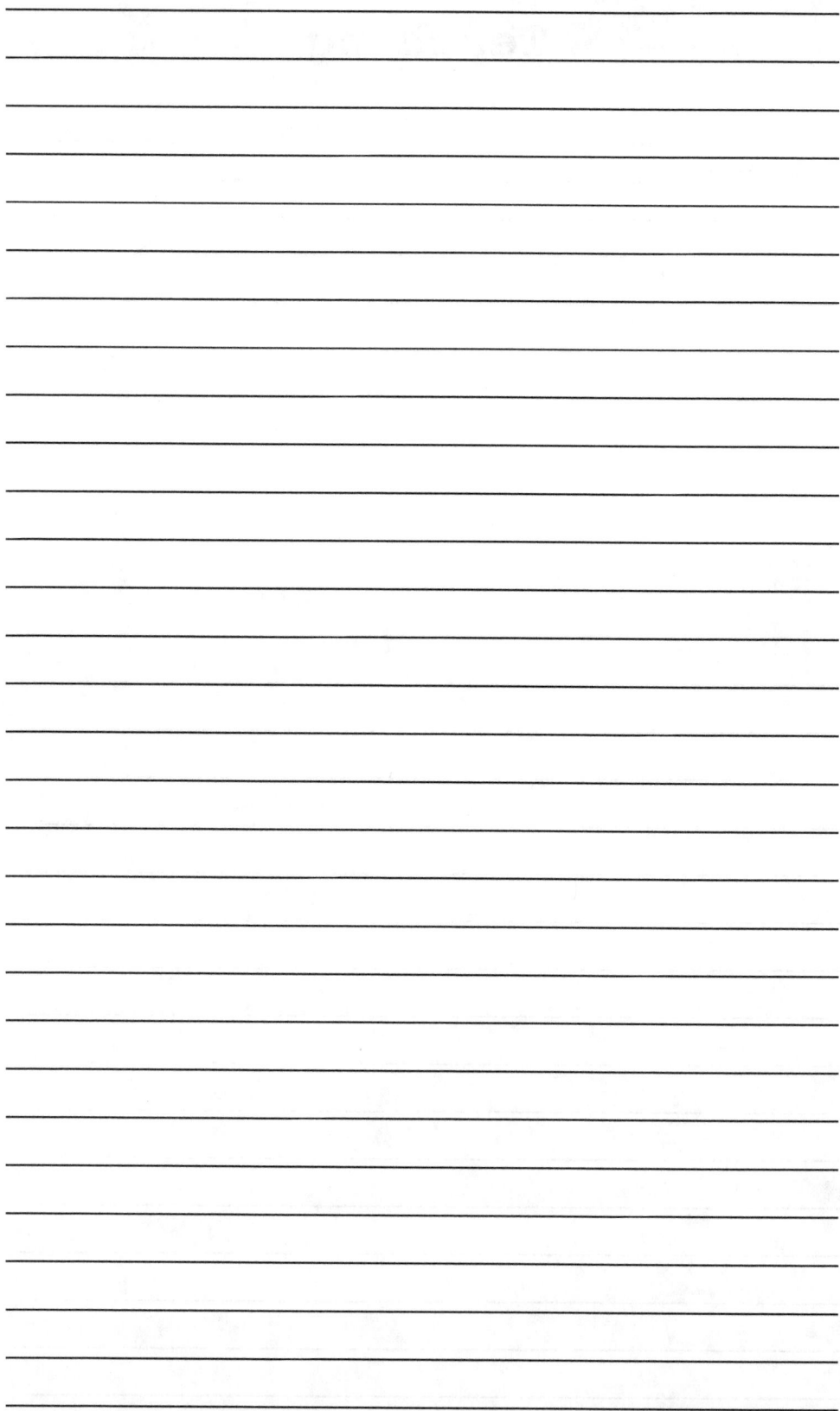

Teaching

Date_____   Speaker_____

Bible Verse _____

Topic _____

_____
_____
_____
_____
_____
_____
_____
_____
_____
_____
_____
_____
_____
_____
_____
_____
_____
_____
_____
_____
_____
_____
_____
_____
_____
_____
_____
_____
_____

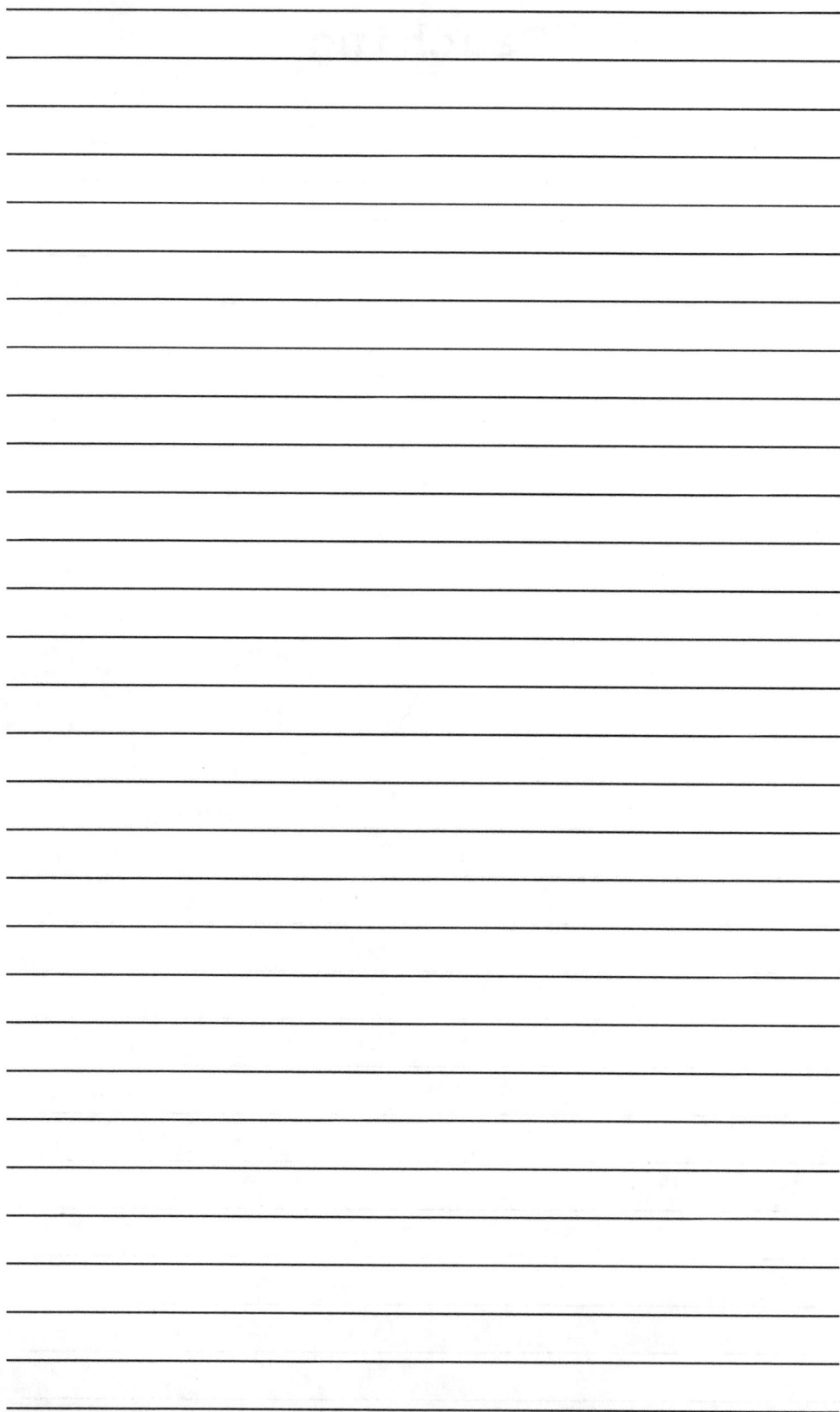

Teaching

Date_____ Speaker_____

Bible Verse _____

Topic _____

_____
_____
_____
_____
_____
_____
_____
_____
_____
_____
_____
_____
_____
_____
_____
_____
_____
_____
_____
_____
_____
_____
_____
_____
_____
_____
_____

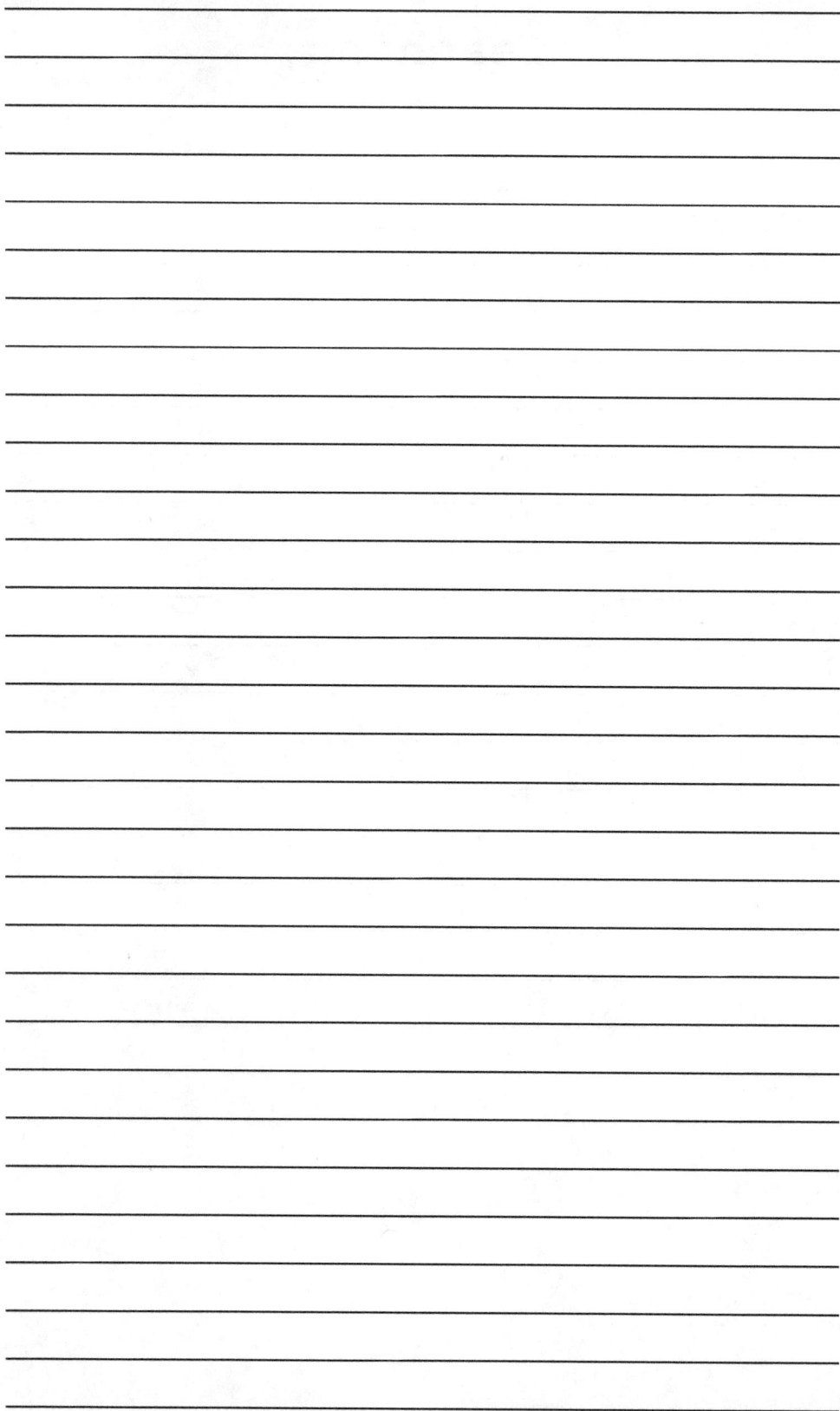

Memory Verse For The Week

_____
_____
_____

_____

My Thoughts Regarding This Verse

_____
_____
_____
_____
_____
_____
_____
_____
_____
_____
_____
_____
_____
_____
_____
_____
_____
_____
_____

Today I Am Grateful For:

_____
_____
_____
_____
_____

Daily Reading

_____
_____
_____
_____
_____
_____
_____
_____

Today's Prayer
Man ought always to pray

_____
_____
_____
_____
_____
_____
_____
_____
_____
_____

Today I Am Grateful For:

_____

_____

_____

_____

_____

Daily Reading

_____

_____

_____

_____

_____

_____

Today's Prayer
Man ought always to pray

_____

_____

_____

_____

_____

_____

_____

_____

Today I Am Grateful For:

_____
_____
_____
_____
_____

Daily Reading

_____
_____
_____
_____
_____
_____
_____

Today's Prayer
Man ought always to pray

_____
_____
_____
_____
_____
_____
_____
_____
_____

Today I Am Grateful For:

_____

_____

_____

_____

_____

Daily Reading

_____

_____

_____

_____

_____

_____

Today's Prayer
Man ought always to pray

_____

_____

_____

_____

_____

_____

_____

_____

_____

Today I Am Grateful For:

_____
_____
_____
_____
_____

Daily Reading

_____
_____
_____
_____
_____
_____
_____

Today's Prayer
Man ought always to pray

_____
_____
_____
_____
_____
_____
_____
_____
_____

Today I Am Grateful For:

_____
_____
_____
_____
_____

Daily Reading

_____
_____
_____
_____
_____
_____
_____

Today's Prayer
Man ought always to pray

_____
_____
_____
_____
_____
_____
_____
_____
_____

Today I Am Grateful For:

_____
_____
_____
_____
_____

Daily Reading

_____
_____
_____
_____
_____
_____
_____
_____

Today's Prayer
Man ought always to pray

_____
_____
_____
_____
_____
_____
_____
_____
_____

Teaching

Date_____   Speaker_____

Bible Verse _____

Topic _____

_____

_____

_____

_____

_____

_____

_____

_____

_____

_____

_____

_____

_____

_____

_____

_____

_____

_____

_____

_____

_____

_____

_____

_____

_____

_____

_____

_____

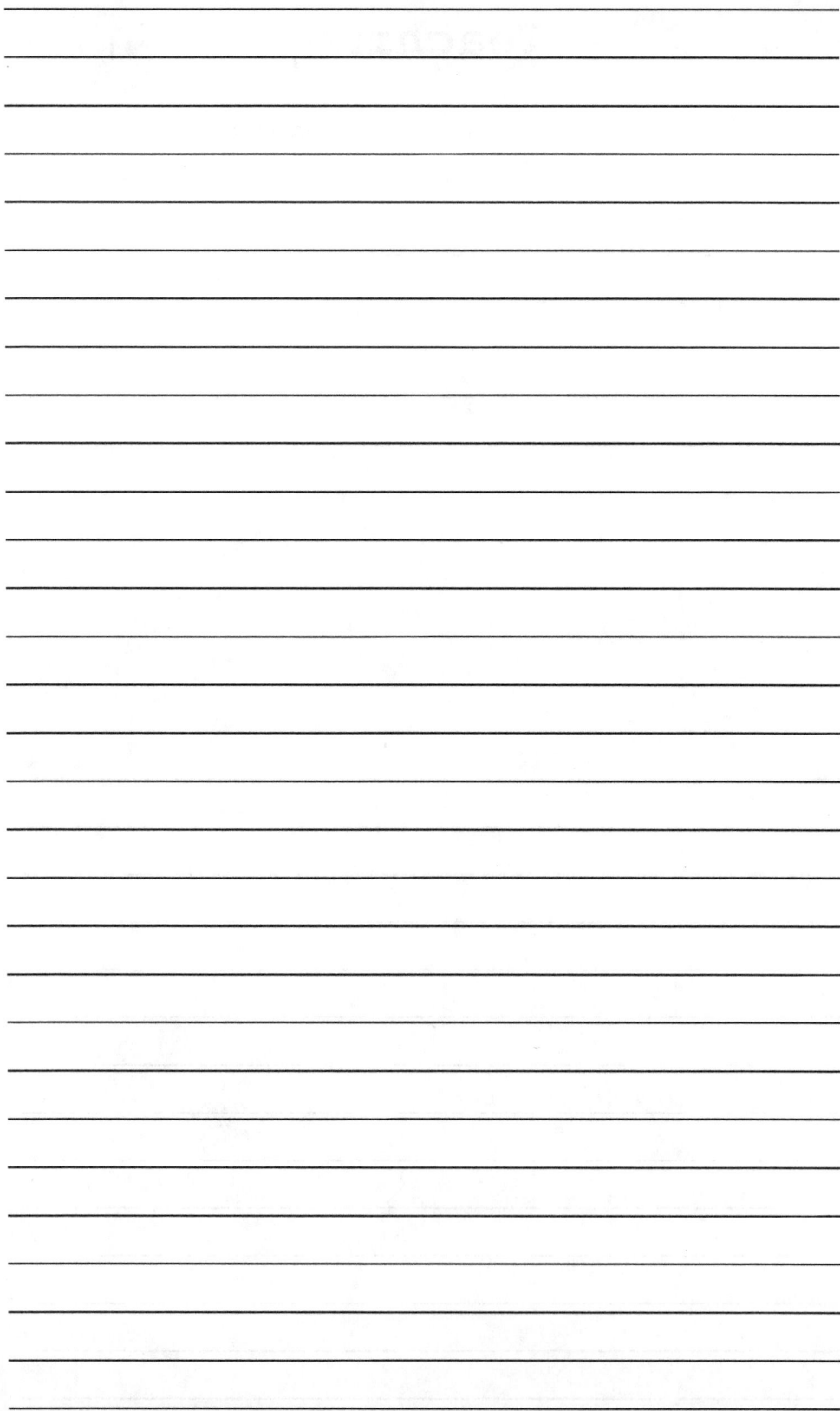

Teaching

Date_____   Speaker_____

Bible Verse _____

Topic _____

_____
_____
_____
_____
_____
_____
_____
_____
_____
_____
_____
_____
_____
_____
_____
_____
_____
_____
_____
_____
_____
_____
_____
_____
_____
_____
_____

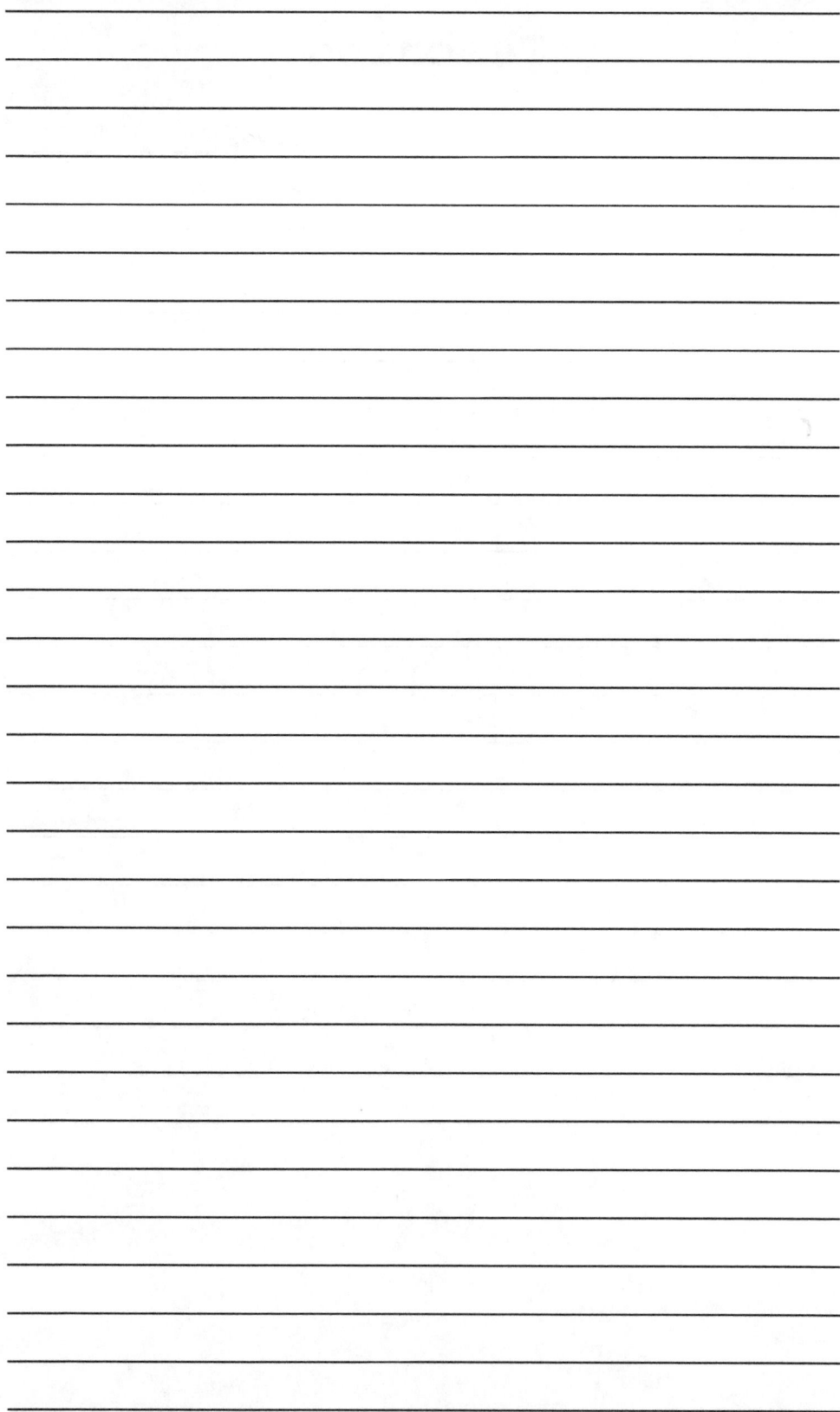

Teaching

Date_____   Speaker_____

Bible Verse _____

Topic _____

_____
_____
_____
_____
_____
_____
_____
_____
_____
_____
_____
_____
_____
_____
_____
_____
_____
_____
_____
_____
_____
_____
_____
_____
_____
_____
_____
_____

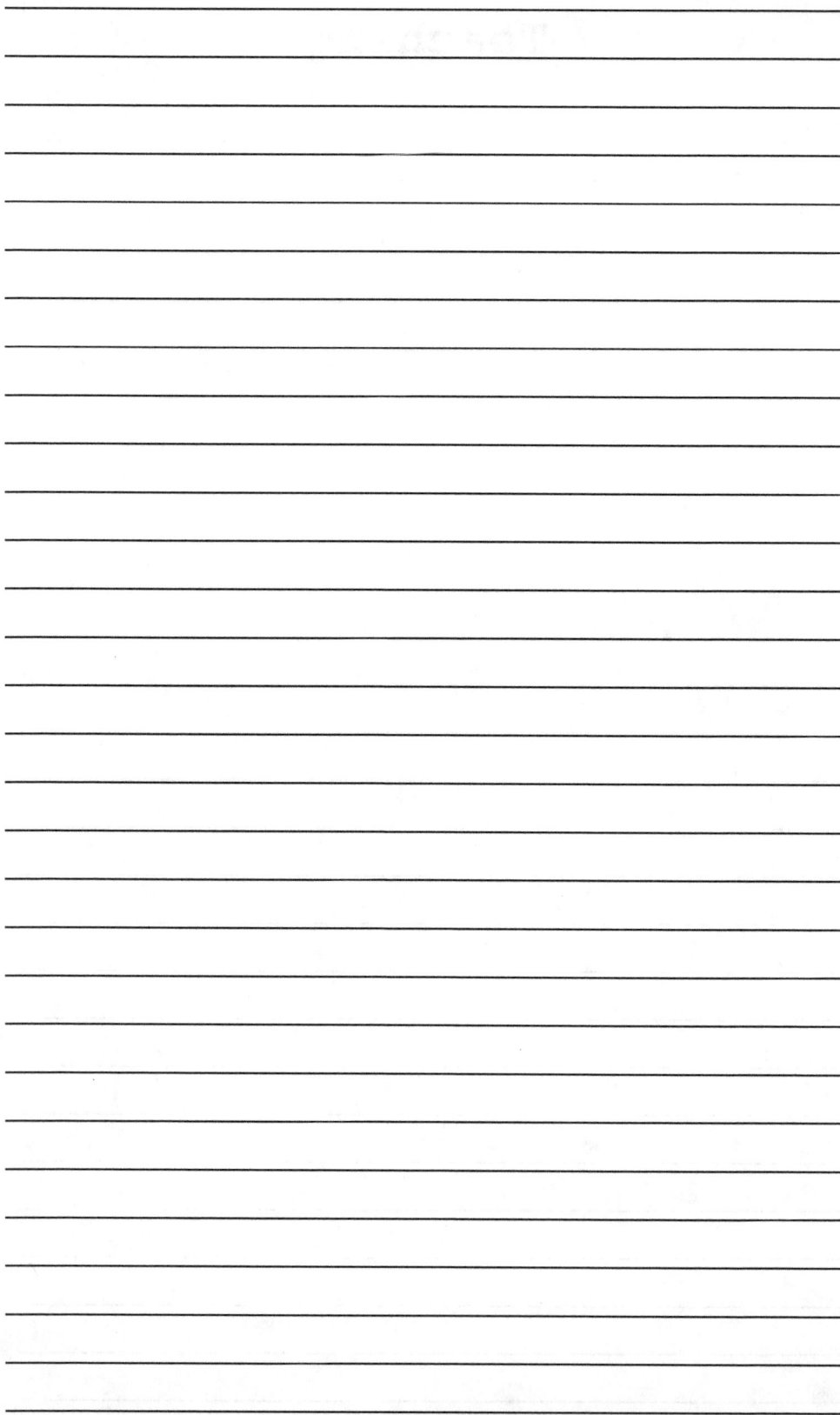

Date: _____

Memory Verse For The Week

_____

_____

_____

_____

My Thoughts Regarding This Verse

_____

_____

_____

_____

_____

_____

_____

_____

_____

_____

_____

_____

_____

_____

_____

_____

_____

_____

_____

_____

Today I Am Grateful For:

_____

_____

_____

_____

_____

Daily Reading

_____

_____

_____

_____

_____

_____

_____

Today's Prayer
Man ought always to pray

_____

_____

_____

_____

_____

_____

_____

_____

_____

Today I Am Grateful For:

_____
_____
_____
_____
_____

Daily Reading

_____
_____
_____
_____
_____
_____
_____

Today's Prayer
Man ought always to pray

_____
_____
_____
_____
_____
_____
_____
_____
_____

Today I Am Grateful For:

_____
_____
_____
_____
_____

Daily Reading

_____
_____
_____
_____
_____
_____
_____

Today's Prayer
Man ought always to pray

_____
_____
_____
_____
_____
_____
_____
_____
_____

Today I Am Grateful For:

_____
_____
_____
_____
_____

Daily Reading

_____
_____
_____
_____
_____
_____
_____

Today's Prayer
Man ought always to pray

_____
_____
_____
_____
_____
_____
_____
_____
_____

Today I Am Grateful For:

_____
_____
_____
_____
_____

Daily Reading

_____
_____
_____
_____
_____
_____
_____

Today's Prayer
Man ought always to pray

_____
_____
_____
_____
_____
_____
_____
_____
_____
_____

Today I Am Grateful For:

_____
_____
_____
_____
_____

Daily Reading

_____
_____
_____
_____
_____
_____

Today's Prayer
Man ought always to pray

_____
_____
_____
_____
_____
_____
_____
_____

Today I Am Grateful For:

_____
_____
_____
_____
_____

Daily Reading

_____
_____
_____
_____
_____
_____
_____

Today's Prayer
Man ought always to pray

_____
_____
_____
_____
_____
_____
_____
_____
_____
_____

Teaching

Date_____   Speaker_____

Bible Verse _____

Topic _____

_____
_____
_____
_____
_____
_____
_____
_____
_____
_____
_____
_____
_____
_____
_____
_____
_____
_____
_____
_____
_____
_____
_____
_____
_____
_____
_____
_____

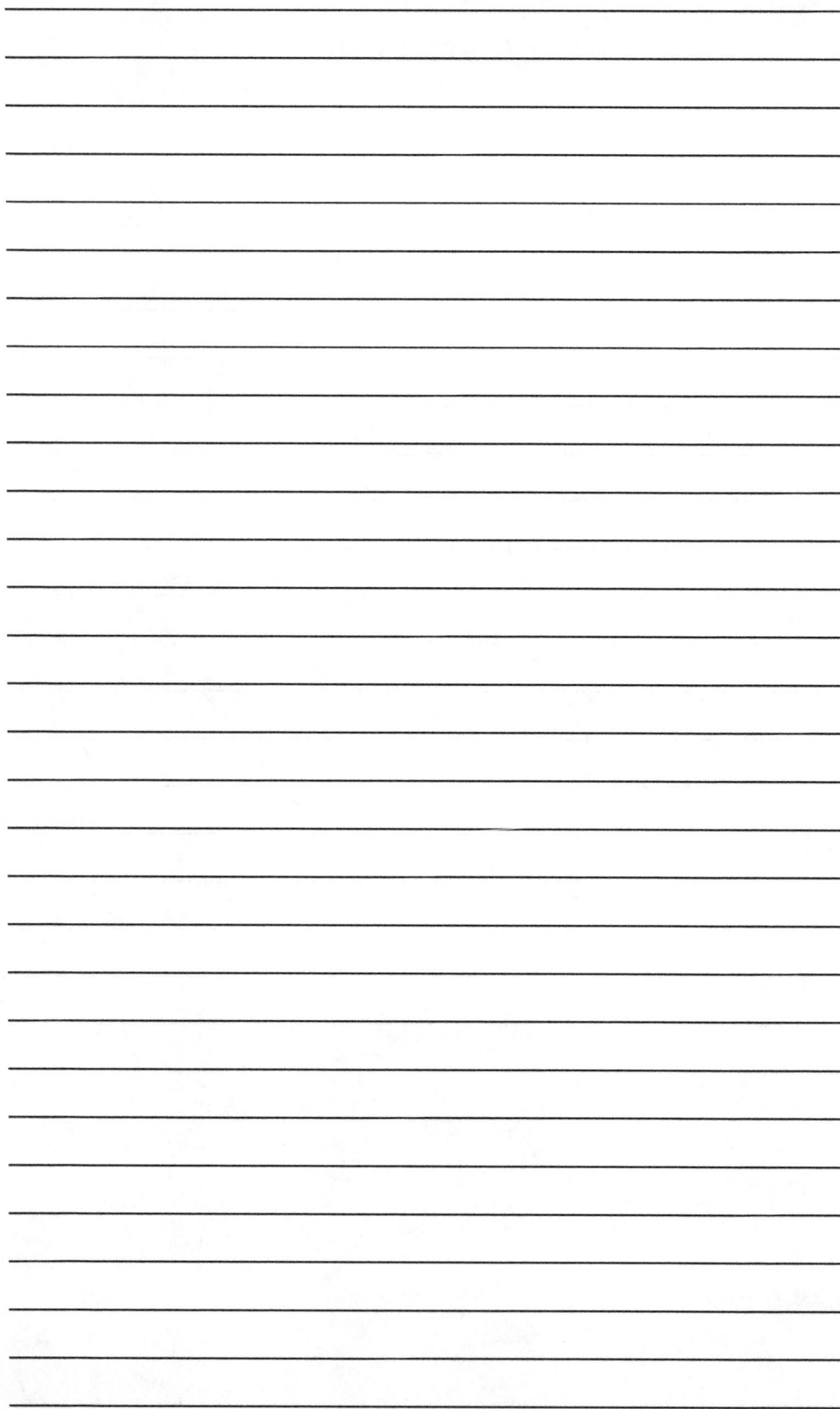

Teaching

Date_____   Speaker_____

Bible Verse _____

Topic _____

_____
_____
_____
_____
_____
_____
_____
_____
_____
_____
_____
_____
_____
_____
_____
_____
_____
_____
_____
_____
_____
_____
_____
_____
_____
_____
_____
_____
_____
_____

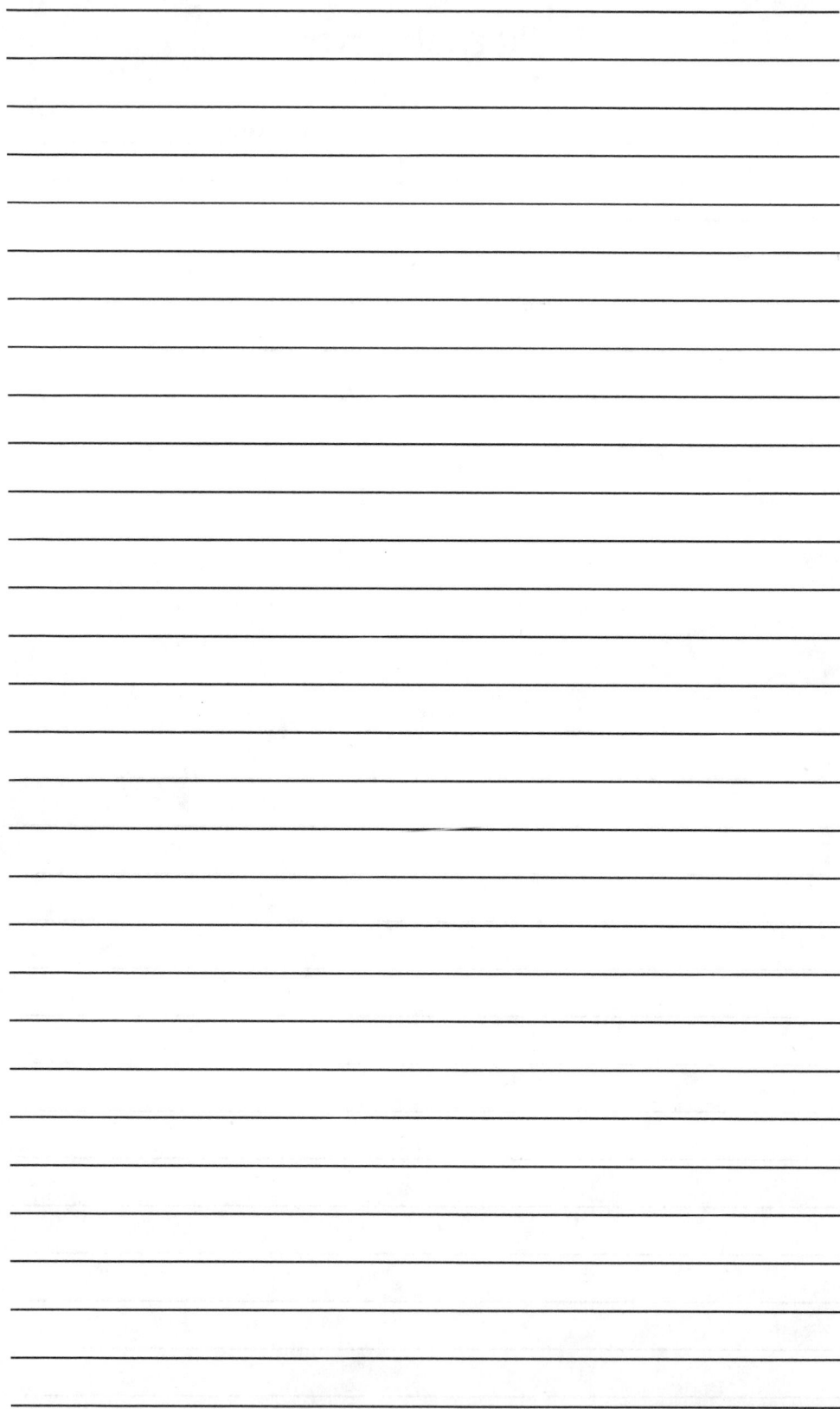

Teaching

Date_____   Speaker_____
Bible Verse _____
Topic _____

_____
_____
_____
_____
_____
_____
_____
_____
_____
_____
_____
_____
_____
_____
_____
_____
_____
_____
_____
_____
_____
_____
_____
_____
_____
_____
_____
_____

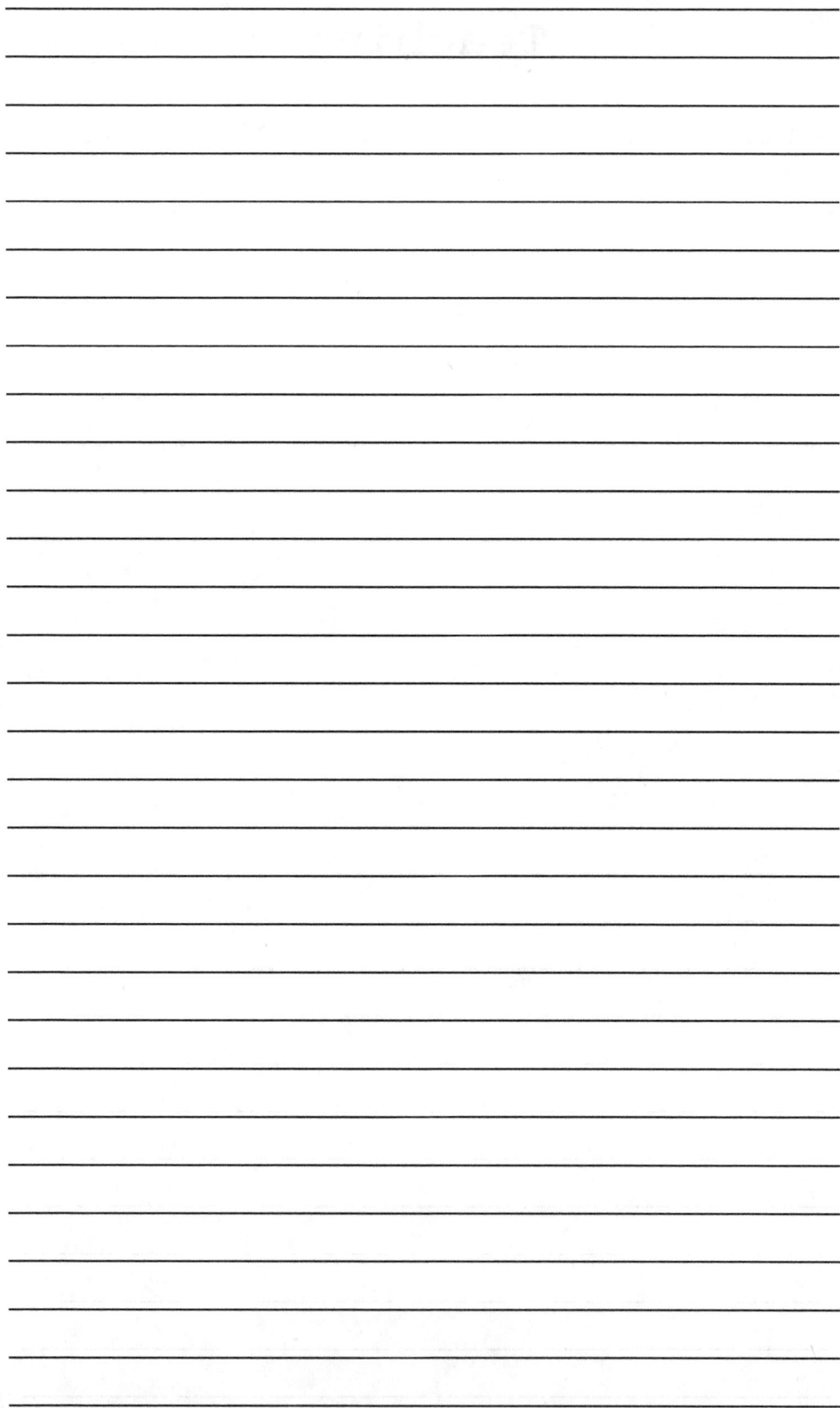

Date: _____

Memory Verse For The Week

_____

_____

_____

_____

My Thoughts Regarding This Verse

_____

_____

_____

_____

_____

_____

_____

_____

_____

_____

_____

_____

_____

_____

_____

_____

_____

_____

_____

_____

_____

Today I Am Grateful For:

_____

_____

_____

_____

_____

Daily Reading

_____

_____

_____

_____

_____

_____

_____

Today's Prayer
Man ought always to pray

_____

_____

_____

_____

_____

_____

_____

_____

_____

Today I Am Grateful For:

_____
_____
_____
_____
_____

Daily Reading

_____
_____
_____
_____
_____
_____

Today's Prayer
Man ought always to pray

_____
_____
_____
_____
_____
_____
_____
_____
_____

Today I Am Grateful For:

_____

_____

_____

_____

_____

Daily Reading

_____

_____

_____

_____

_____

_____

_____

_____

Today's Prayer
Man ought always to pray

_____

_____

_____

_____

_____

_____

_____

_____

_____

_____

Today I Am Grateful For:

_____

_____

_____

_____

_____

Daily Reading

_____

_____

_____

_____

_____

_____

_____

Today's Prayer

Man ought always to pray

_____

_____

_____

_____

_____

_____

_____

_____

Today I Am Grateful For:

_____

_____

_____

_____

_____

Daily Reading

_____

_____

_____

_____

_____

_____

_____

_____

Today's Prayer
Man ought always to pray

_____

_____

_____

_____

_____

_____

_____

_____

_____

Today I Am Grateful For:

_____

_____

_____

_____

_____

Daily Reading

_____

_____

_____

_____

_____

_____

_____

Today's Prayer

Man ought always to pray

_____

_____

_____

_____

_____

_____

_____

_____

_____

Today I Am Grateful For:

_____

_____

_____

_____

_____

Daily Reading

_____

_____

_____

_____

_____

_____

_____

Today's Prayer
Man ought always to pray

_____

_____

_____

_____

_____

_____

_____

_____

_____

Teaching

Date_____   Speaker_____

Bible Verse _____

Topic _____

_____

_____

_____

_____

_____

_____

_____

_____

_____

_____

_____

_____

_____

_____

_____

_____

_____

_____

_____

_____

_____

_____

_____

_____

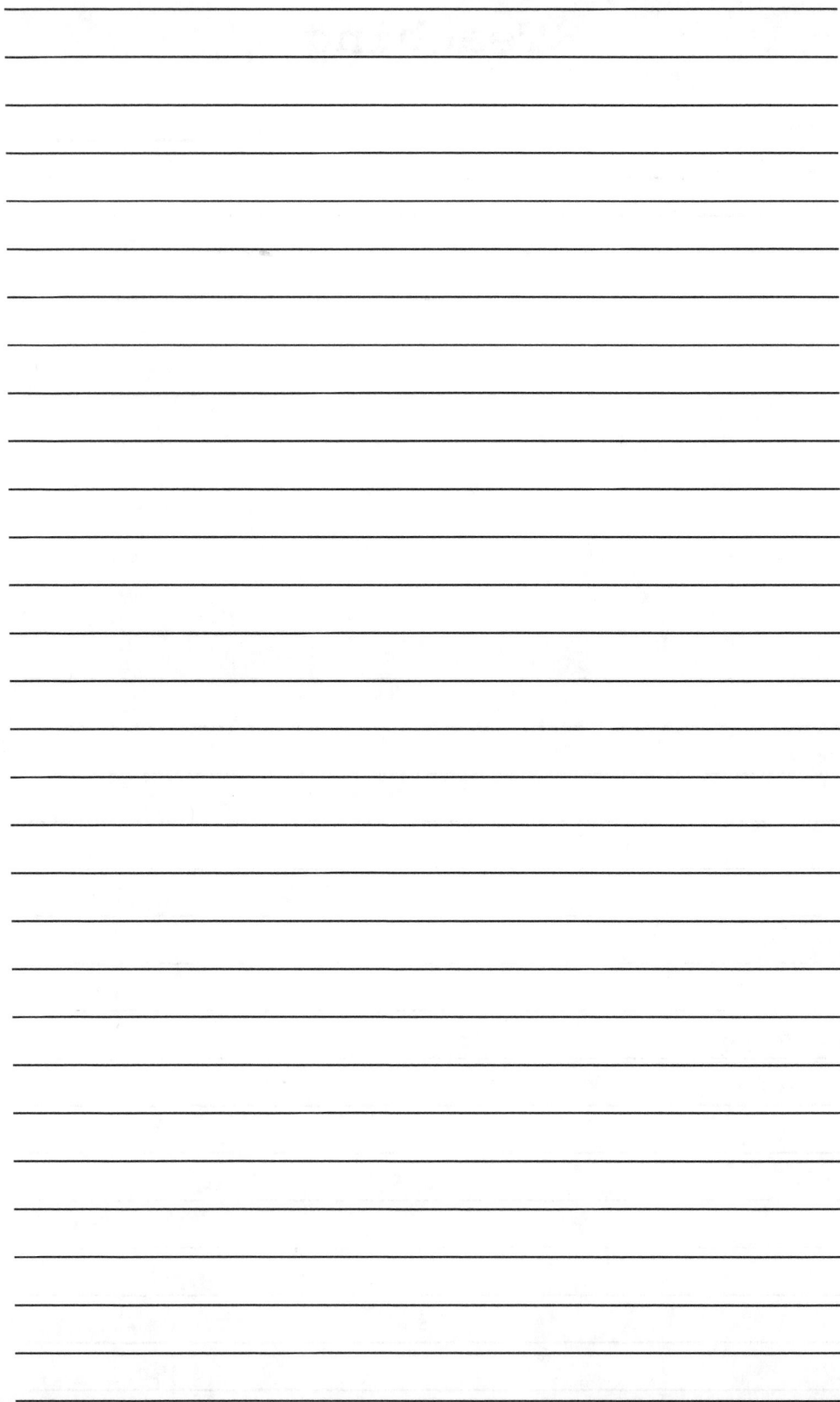

Teaching

Date_____   Speaker_____

Bible Verse _____

Topic _____

_____
_____
_____
_____
_____
_____
_____
_____
_____
_____
_____
_____
_____
_____
_____
_____
_____
_____
_____
_____
_____
_____
_____
_____
_____
_____
_____
_____
_____
_____
_____
_____
_____

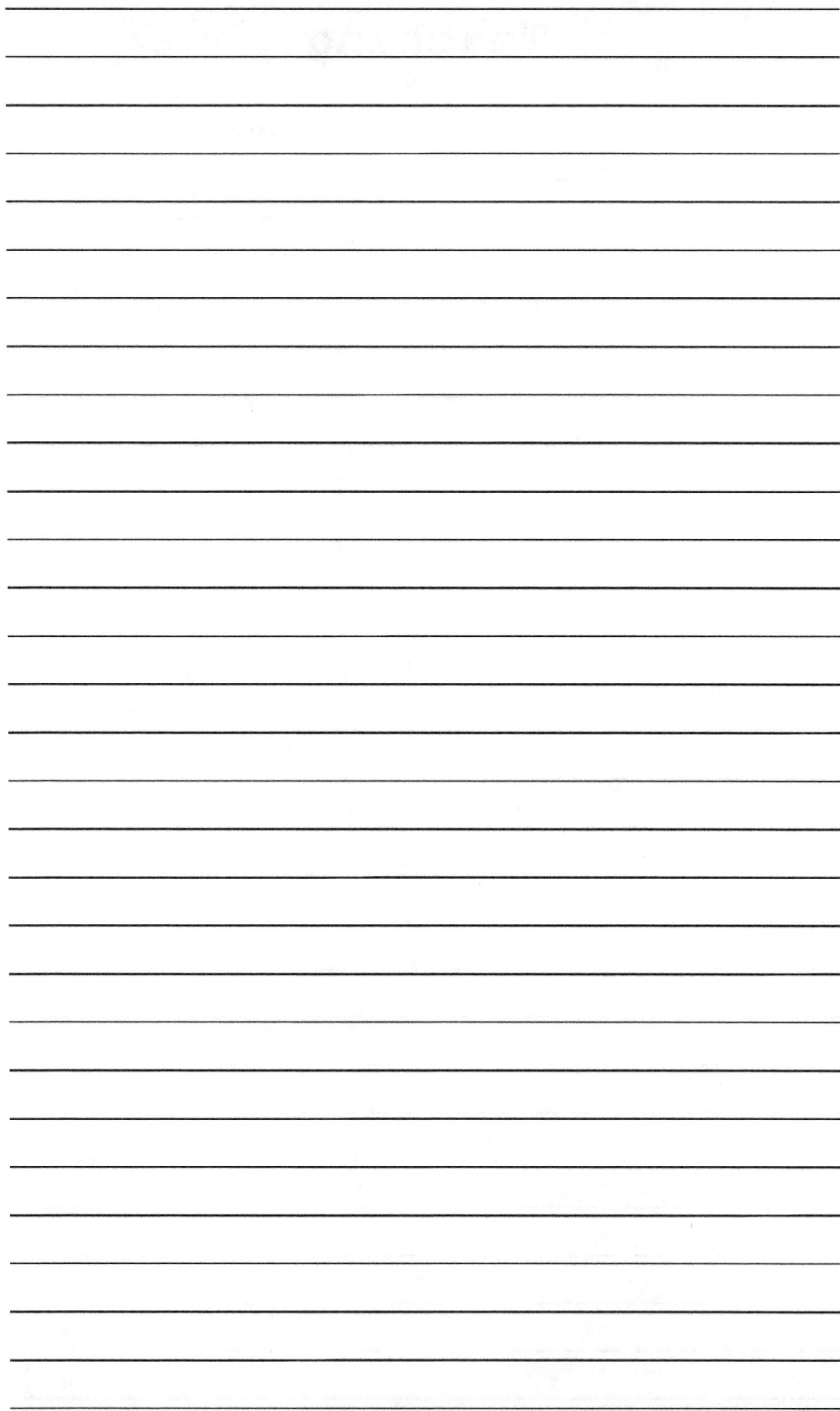

Teaching

Date_____   Speaker_____

Bible Verse _____

Topic _____

_____
_____
_____
_____
_____
_____
_____
_____
_____
_____
_____
_____
_____
_____
_____
_____
_____
_____
_____
_____
_____
_____
_____
_____
_____
_____
_____
_____

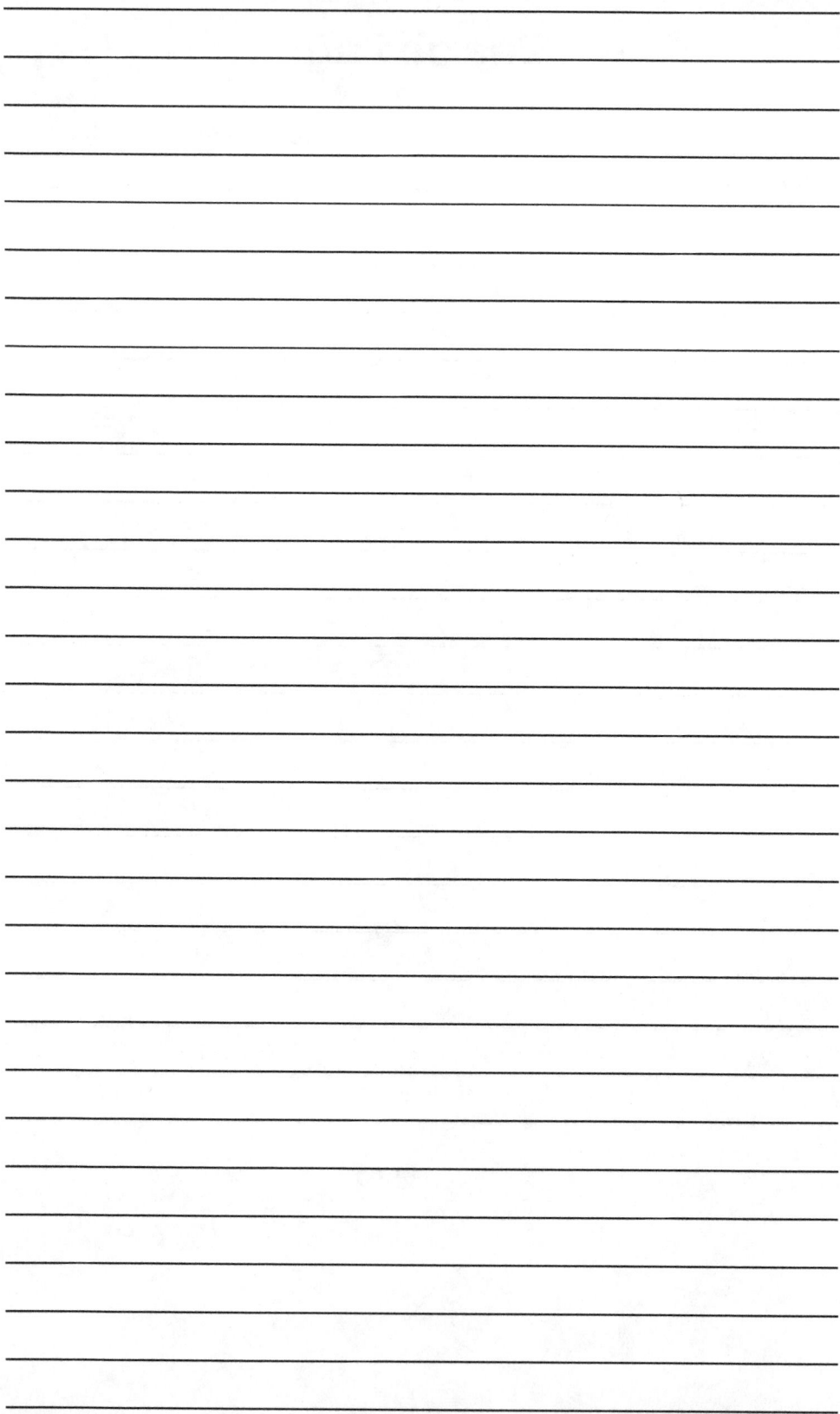

Date: _____

Memory Verse For The Week

_____
_____
_____
_____

My Thoughts Regarding This Verse

_____
_____
_____
_____
_____
_____
_____
_____
_____
_____
_____
_____
_____
_____
_____
_____
_____
_____
_____
_____

Today I Am Grateful For:

_____

_____

_____

_____

_____

Daily Reading

_____

_____

_____

_____

_____

_____

_____

_____

Today's Prayer
Man ought always to pray

_____

_____

_____

_____

_____

_____

_____

_____

_____

_____

Today I Am Grateful For:

_____
_____
_____
_____
_____

Daily Reading

_____
_____
_____
_____
_____
_____
_____

Today's Prayer
Man ought always to pray

_____
_____
_____
_____
_____
_____
_____
_____

Today I Am Grateful For:

_____
_____
_____
_____
_____

Daily Reading

_____
_____
_____
_____
_____
_____
_____
_____

Today's Prayer
Man ought always to pray

_____
_____
_____
_____
_____
_____
_____
_____
_____
_____
_____

Today I Am Grateful For:

Daily Reading

Today's Prayer
Man ought always to pray

Today I Am Grateful For:

_____
_____
_____
_____
_____

Daily Reading

_____
_____
_____
_____
_____
_____
_____
_____

Today's Prayer
Man ought always to pray

_____
_____
_____
_____
_____
_____
_____
_____
_____
_____

Today I Am Grateful For:

_____
_____
_____
_____
_____

Daily Reading

_____
_____
_____
_____
_____
_____
_____

Today's Prayer
Man ought always to pray

_____
_____
_____
_____
_____
_____
_____
_____

Today I Am Grateful For:

_____
_____
_____
_____
_____

Daily Reading

_____
_____
_____
_____
_____
_____
_____
_____

Today's Prayer
Man ought always to pray

_____
_____
_____
_____
_____
_____
_____
_____
_____
_____

Teaching

Date_____ Speaker_____

Bible Verse _____

Topic _____

_____

_____

_____

_____

_____

_____

_____

_____

_____

_____

_____

_____

_____

_____

_____

_____

_____

_____

_____

_____

_____

_____

_____

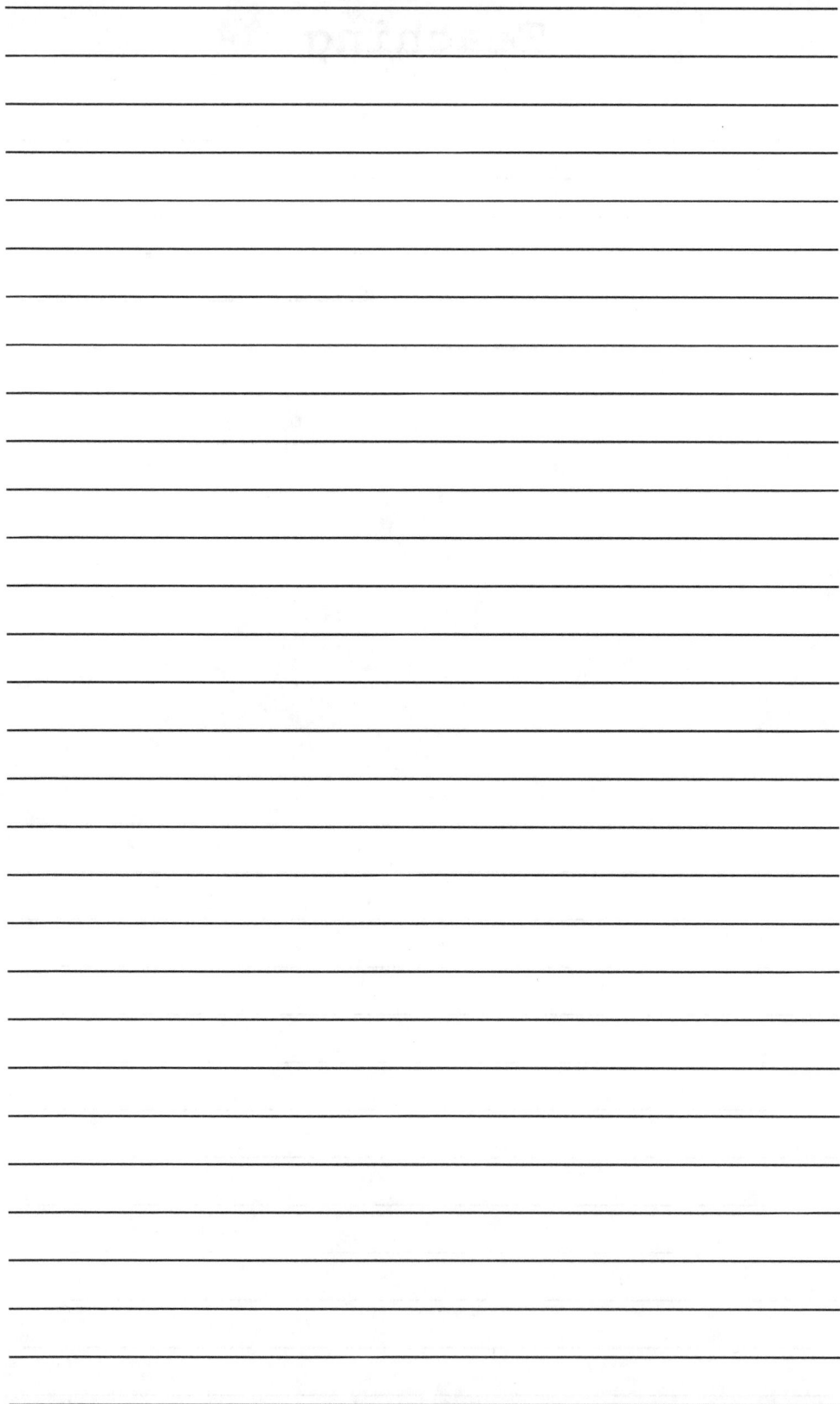

Teaching

Date_____   Speaker_____

Bible Verse _____

Topic _____

_____
_____
_____
_____
_____
_____
_____
_____
_____
_____
_____
_____
_____
_____
_____
_____
_____
_____
_____
_____
_____
_____
_____
_____
_____
_____
_____
_____
_____

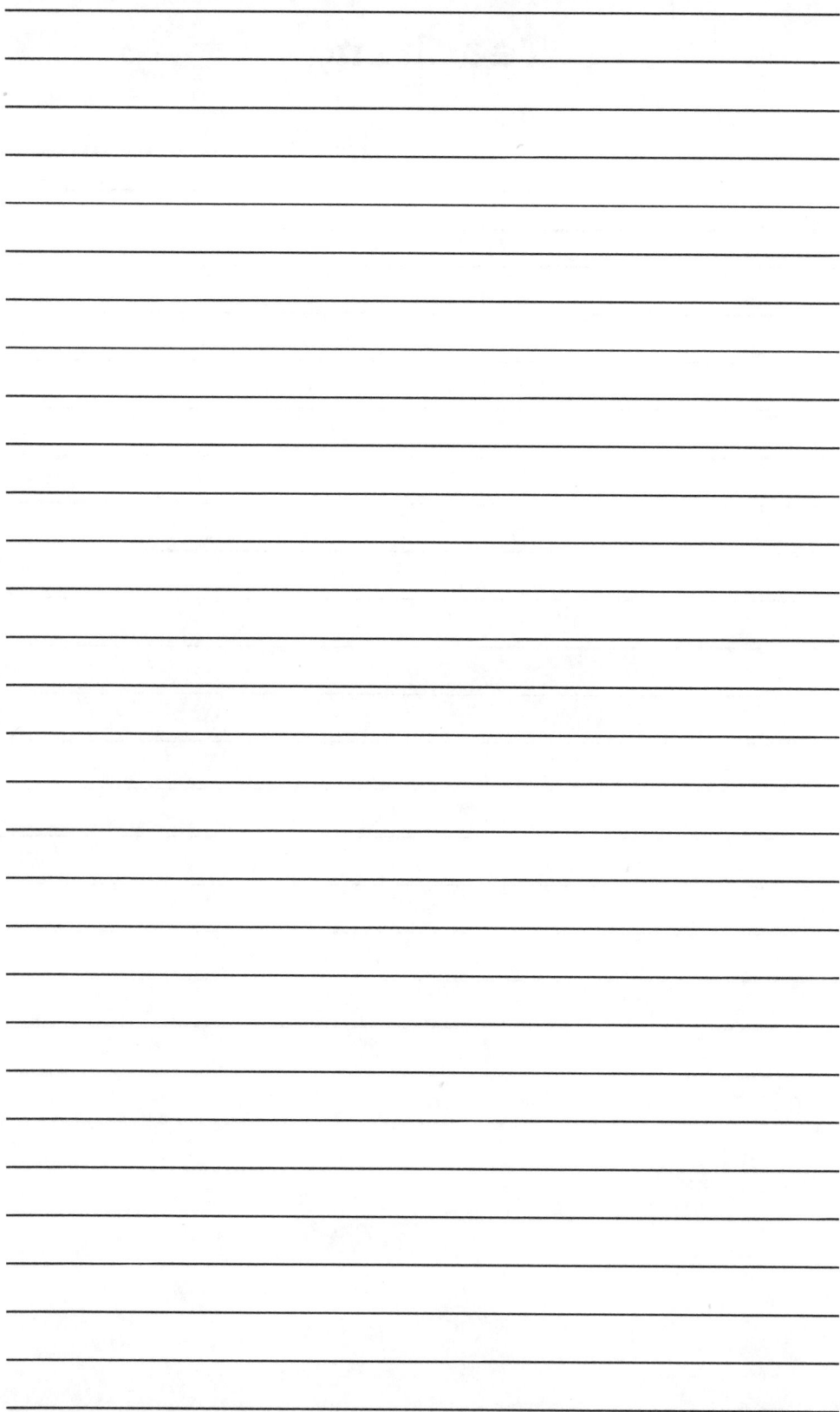

Teaching

Date_____   Speaker_____

Bible Verse _____

Topic _____

_____
_____
_____
_____
_____
_____
_____
_____
_____
_____
_____
_____
_____
_____
_____
_____
_____
_____
_____
_____
_____
_____
_____
_____
_____
_____
_____

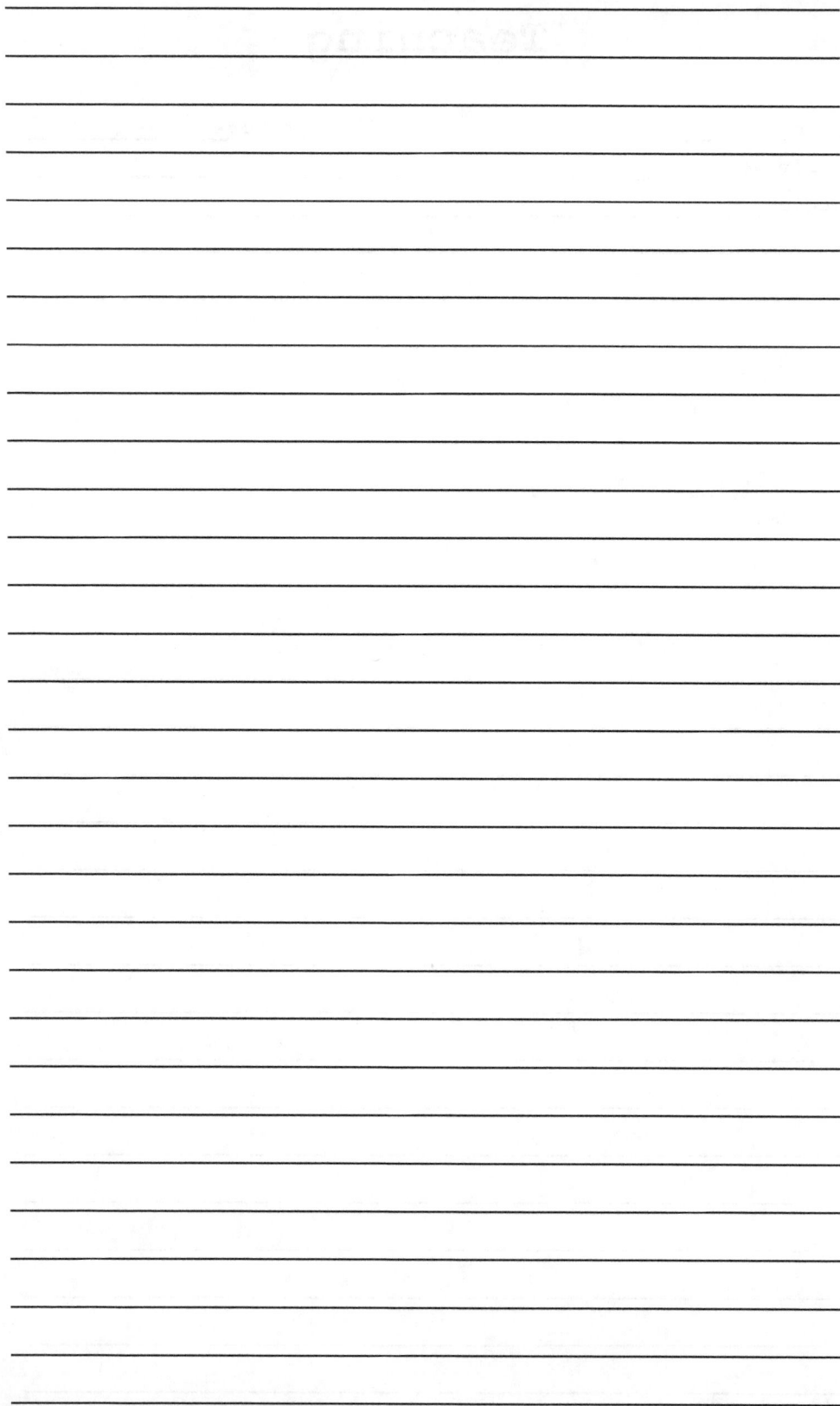

Reflections

As I reflect on this season in my life, these are my thoughts

_____

_____

_____

_____

_____

_____

_____

_____

_____

_____

_____

_____

_____

_____

_____

_____

_____

_____

_____

_____

_____

_____

_____

_____

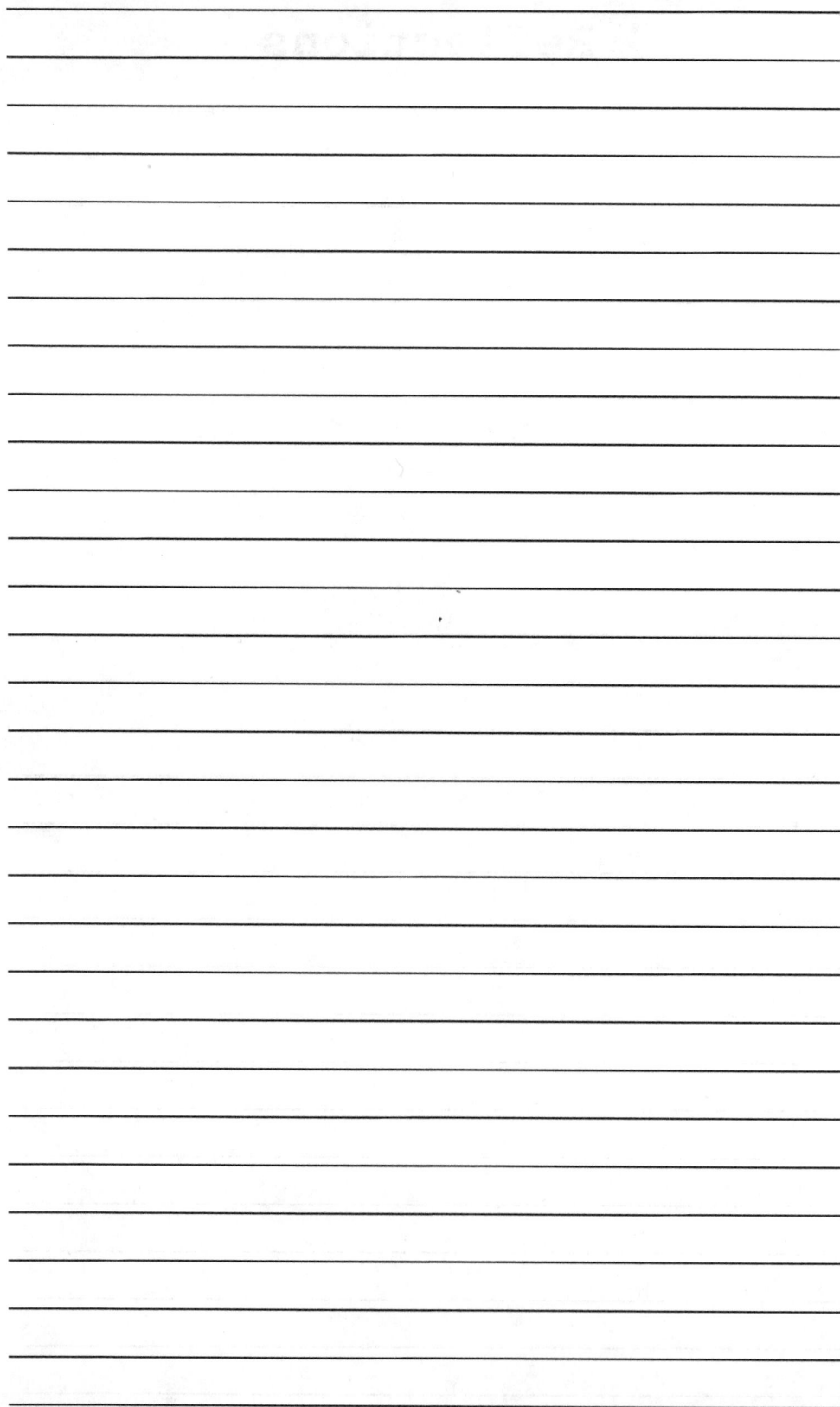

www.ingramcontent.com/pod-product-compliance
Lightning Source LLC
Chambersburg PA
CBHW051041030426
42339CB00006B/144